Burnt Offerings

A Collection of Recipes by Priests and Bishops of the Archdiocese of Chicago and Beyond

Compiled by Rev. Ken Fleck

ISBN: 0-9790375-0-6
978-0-9790375-0-4

Dedication

This cookbook is the result of almost twelve years of collecting recipes from priests and bishops, even writing twice to the pope. One of the Vatican responses is contained along with the picture of Pope John Paul II.

The purpose of the book is twofold. I love to cook, bake, prepare food, and enjoy sharing food with family and friends. Meals should be more than refueling stops for the body. Meals are times to feed the soul with the blessings reflected upon, to nourish the emotions with good conversation, and to renew the spirit with the encouragement and excitement of stories shared. Mealtime is a creative time. These are lessons I've learned from my family while growing up at Sacred Heart Church at 70th and May Streets.

The second purpose of this book is to dispel the myth and mystery that sometimes surround priests as a "breed apart". We are called and respond from the midst of our communities. We lead prayer, preach, celebrate the sacraments, visit the sick, comfort the dying, counsel the troubled, and at times trouble the conscience. We enjoy watching sports, playing sports, going on picnics, taking vacations, going to plays, movies, and museums. While we do not have wives and children, we share in the joy of watching "our children" grow up from the time we baptize some to when we solemnize their marriages. We rejoice in their accomplishments and share in their defeats. Like all good parents we have the power both to forgive mistakes and to encourage the right behavior. We lead by example as well as by word. We have our dreams, our fears, and our nightmares.

I hope that those who try the recipes in this book, representing a wide variety of priests including three popes, will be able to reflect on the good priests who are ordinary guys with an extraordinary dream. With their faults and failings, skills and talents they seek to answer the call heard long ago to help and serve—to be Christ for others.

It is my wish that other young men will hear the call to serve as priests, receive the encouragement we had in our early years, and generously say "Yes" to the Lord. It is a wonderful way to live a fulfilling life. The sacrifice that is called for in a priest is the same sacrifice a person makes in marriage: commitment—for better or worse, for richer or poorer, in sickness and in health, all the days of your life.

The real challenge is not in finding vocations. The call of the Lord is present in the needs around us. The answer lies in the hearts of our children. The challenge is whether or not we believe enough in the good news of the Kingdom of God to let our children respond by talking to them about vocations to religious life.

I thank God for the love of my mother and her guidance in the kitchen. And I am thankful that my siblings and I helped with the kitchen chores. We all learned well. I thank God for my sister who, being the only girl with four older brothers and being born on Christmas day, robbed me of my baby position in the family. Her arrival forced me to fight for attention by helping Mom in the kitchen. I thank God for my father. His stories inspired me to make exploding root beer, make wine from grape juice, try my hand at baking, and not be afraid of trying new things. I am grateful to both my parents for teaching us the lesson of giving without asking what was in it for me and of knowing that the Lord saw in secret and would reward us.

I thank God for all the family members and parishioners who gave me encouragement and hope along the way from seminary days working in apostolates, to my diaconate at St. Bride (78th St. and Coles Ave.), my first parish at St. Felicitas (84th St. and Blackstone) as associate and administrator, and my first pastorate at Our Lady of Peace (79th St. and Jeffrey Blvd.) where the dream of this cookbook was born in a musing moment late at night. I had wonderful volunteers who helped type drafts, forge ideas, and challenge me to go beyond priests to bishops, cardinals and even the pope! At St. Barnabas (101st St. and Longwood Drive) I came to experience priesthood as an associate again enjoying the opportunities of being present to parishioners with a message of hope. They too kept the dream of my cookbook alive. Here I came across Ralph Smith who did much of the artwork along with Bill Porcelli. Peggy and Rosemary DuMais helped with the second draft and the final translation of the manuscript from a Word document to a Publisher's document. St. Jude in South Holland was a ten month period in my ministry which was a creative step. Fr. Tom Cabala, their pastor, gave me ribbing as well as support. My current assignment, as pastor of St. George in Tinley Park, made me realize I had to finish this creative work. Roman Wojcik put in endless hours with his skills at pixel art, cleaning up drawings, and tediously attending to detail with his computer skills to make the final draft a reality. Each parish provided numerous volunteers to help read and make suggestions and corrections.

At each parish I had the opportunity to teach young and old alike the joys of cooking and baking and spending time in the kitchen together. Time is the most precious gift we have in this life. It cannot be purchased. Each person has the same twenty-four hours to spend as he/she wishes. I treasure the childhood memories I have of time spent cracking nuts, peeling apples, and even washing dishes. The first language each of us learns is sign language as babies. Many lessons were learned through the silent sign language of sharing, spending time with family and friends. We even used words for some lessons. I passed those same lessons along in my own way to those who came in the kitchen and wanted to learn more than an art of baking, but lessons in life. I learned from them as well.

I am indebted to all who helped and encouraged me along the way. Now it is your turn to take time, to teach, to learn, and to be creative.

Fr. Ken Fleck

PREFACE

A True Story of an Untrue Revelation

For years I have denied what family, friends, and parishioners have been telling me. I hoped it wasn't true, but then, how did others come to know *they* were chosen.

The first few times it happened, I thought it was a slip of the tongue, a mistake, a careless phrase. But as many more used the phrase, I had to face the reality of what they were saying. What else could it be? It was said by my family who knew me as "Ken". It was said by friends who had called me "Ken" for years. I was acknowledged even by parishioners who had seen my name printed in the bulletins—"Fr. Ken Fleck" and by some who had called me "'Pa' Fleck". But it has been repeated again and again. How could I deny what they were saying?

I was helping a friend and her husband move into their apartment. It was a winter day in January. As I carried a box of books in my arms, my friend opened the heavy outer door to let me in. It slipped from her hand and hit me square in the forehead. She blurted out, "God, are you okay?" I dismissed it.

That same week, on Sunday after Mass, I went outside on the front porch of Our Lady of Peace church in my vestments to greet the parishioners and wish them a blessed day. I slipped on a patch of ice and was knocked off my feet. Many of the parishioners said, "My God, are you alright?"

Even my own family, remarking on my humor, have said, "God, do you tell bad jokes!"

Thus the story of creation as told in this book through the eyes of a priest masquerading as a chef.

Fr. Ken Fleck

SECRETARIAT OF STATE

FIRST SECTION - GENERAL AFFAIRS

From the Vatican, December 4, 1995

Dear Father Fleck,

I am directed to acknowledge your letter of May 31, 1995. I regret that the vast amount of mail has made an earlier reply impossible.

In this regard, I must inform you that it is not possible to comply with your request for a recipe recommended by the Holy Father.

At the same time I am pleased to convey His Holiness's prayerful good wishes for your efforts.

Sincerely yours in Christ,

Monsignor L. Sandri
Assessor

The Reverend Kenneth J. Fleck
Pastor
Our Lady of Peace Parish
7851 S. Jeffery Blvd.
Chicago, IL   60649-5028

His Holiness, Pope John Paul II

Day One

How it All Got Started

The Big Bang Theory of Creation

Appetizers

Al's Appetizers

1 c. sharp cheddar cheese, grated
1/2 t. dry mustard
1 dash Tabasco sauce
1/4 t. Worcestershire sauce
1 whole egg
Cocktail Rounds or Triscuit crackers

Combine cheese, mustard, Tabasco and Worcestershire sauces, and egg in a bowl and beat until light and fluffy. Toast buttered rounds on one side. With a teaspoon cover toasted round with cheese mixture. Place on a cookie sheet under broiler until lightly browned. (about 2 minutes at 4 inches)

Variation
1 c. finely shredded cheddar cheese
1/2 c. finely diced onion
1/2 c. mayo or Miracle whip
1/2 t. garlic salt or seasoned salt

Spread on your favorite cracker. Place on a cookie sheet under broiler for 60 to 90 seconds to heat mixture. Serve hot.

Rev. Ken Fleck

Angels in Blankets

36 shrimp or less
18 slices of bacon cut in half
Dijon mustard

Spread each of 18 bacon slices, cut in half, with about one half teaspoon prepared mustard. Wrap shrimp in prepared bacon slice and secure with toothpick. Preheat broiler for 5 minutes. Broil shrimp six inches from heat for 3 to 4 minutes. Turn and broil 2 to 3 minutes more. Serve hot.

Rev. Richard Ehrens

Sweet 'N' Sour Chicken Wings

6 chicken wings per person
1/8 c. peach preserves
1/4 c. Original Open Pit Bar B Q Sauce

Cut bony part of chicken wing off so that wings resemble mini chicken legs. Save these parts for later soup stock. Mix preserves and sauce. Spread over mini chicken drumsticks. Place upon cookie sheet lined with aluminum foil for easy clean-up. Bake uncovered at 350 degrees for 30 minutes.

Rev. Jerry Rodell

Archdiocesan Dip

1 c. mayonnaise
1 c. sour cream
1-1/2 c. shredded cheddar cheese
1/2 t. garlic powder
1/4 t. salt
1 t. parsley, chopped

Combine ingredients. Chill overnight. Serve on crackers, or as a dip for vegetables. Makes 4 cups.

Rev. Maurice Kissane

Christine's Christmas Cheese Ball

2 (8 oz.) pkg. cream cheese, room temperature
1 (4 to 5 oz.) pkg. Buddig corn beef
7 green onions, chopped
7 dashes of garlic salt
1 T. mayonnaise
1 t. lemon juice

Mix all ingredients together in a bowl. Shape into a ball or press into a mold that is lined with plastic wrap or lightly greased with a vegetable oil spray so that it will come out easily. Refrigerate for at least one hour. This can be made ahead of time and frozen for up to two months.

Rev. Ken Fleck

Cheese Squares

1 loaf white bread, unsliced
2 egg whites, beaten stiff
1 stick butter
1/4 c. cheddar cheese, shredded
1/4 c. Swiss cheese, shredded
1/4 c. Mozzarella cheese, shredded
8 oz. cream cheese, diced
1/2 t. dry mustard
Dash of cayenne pepper

Melt butter in a saucepan; add cheeses. Heat on low flame till melted and smooth. Add mustard and pepper. Fold in egg whites. Cut bread into one inch cubes. Dip cubes into cheese mixture till coated all over. Place in plastic bags till needed. When ready to serve, bake on ungreased cookie sheet for 10 to 15 minutes at 400 degrees. Will be golden brown. Good snack or appetizer.

Rev. Jerry Williams, O. Carm.

Liver Sausage Dip

1 lb. liver sausage
1 8 oz. pkg. cream cheese
1/3 c. finely chopped dill pickle
1/4 c. minced onion
1/4 c. mayonnaise or salad dressing
2 t. dill pickle juice
1 t. Worcestershire sauce
1/4 t. garlic salt
3 or more drops hot pepper sauce (optional)

With a mixer beat sausage with cream cheese. Add remaining ingredients and beat together well. Line a 3 cup mixing bowl with foil or a mold with plastic wrap. Chill for several hours or overnight.

Serve on a plate surrounded by your favorite crackers.

Rev. Ken Fleck

Hot Artichoke Cheese Dip

Saint James Special

8-1/2 oz. artichoke hearts, drained
6 oz. jar marinated artichoke hearts, drained
4 oz. diced green chilies
6 T. mayonnaise
1-1/2 to 2 c. shredded cheddar cheese
tortilla chips

Chop the artichokes, mix, and distribute evenly over the bottom of a well-greased shallow 2 qt. baking dish. (or a 7-1/2x11 inch baking dish) Scatter the chilies on top, then carefully spread the mayonnaise over all. Sprinkle with the cheese. Cover and chill if made ahead. Bake 350 degree pre-heated oven for 15 minutes (30 if cold). Serve with chips. Makes 2-1/2 cups.

Rev. Bill Zavaski

Cranberry Salsa

2 c. cranberries, coarsely chopped
1/4 c. honey
3 T. fresh cilantro, chopped
3 T. orange juice
1 Serrano chili pepper, seeded, membrane removed, minced
1 T. grated orange rind
1 T. tequila
2 t. grated fresh ginger
1/4 t. ground cumin

Mix all ingredients in medium bowl. Refrigerate covered until ready to use.

Rev. Ron Gollatz

Sausage Appetizers

1 lb. sausage meat
1 lb. ground beef
1 lb. Velveeta cheese
1 t. sweet basil
1 t. oregano
1/2 t. garlic powder
2 t. dried parsley flakes
2 loaves party rye bread

Brown the hamburger and sausage; drain off grease. Cut cheese and add to meat. Stir until cheese is melted. Add seasonings; mix well. Keep mixture on low heat. Spoon onto party rye bread, and put on cookie sheet. Set under broiler till lightly browned. (May be spread on bread and frozen until ready for use.)

Archbishop James Patrick Keleher
Archbishop of Kansas City

Pickled Shrimp

1 c. olive oil
1-1/2 c. white vinegar
1/2 c. honey
1/2 c. fresh lime juice
2 t. celery seeds
salt to taste
2 t. Tabasco sauce
2 med. yellow onions, sliced thin and separated into rings
2 lbs. med. shrimp, cleaned, deveined, just barely cooked

Mix all but shrimp together. Cook shrimp and pour sauce over and refrigerate. Great summer appetizer.

Rev. Jerry Williams, O. Carm.

Shrimp Dip

(For shrimp, crabmeat and lobster)

2 c. mayonnaise or salad dressing
1-1/2 T. dill pickle, finely chopped
1-1/2 T. stuffed olives, finely chopped
1-1/2 T. green pepper, finely chopped
1-1/2 T. parsley, finely chopped
1-1/2 T. chives, finely chopped
1 t. seasoned salt
2 eggs, hard boiled, chopped
4 T. chili sauce

Mix all ingredients together. Place in a small serving bowl with cooked shrimp hanging from the side or surrounding the bowl.

Garnish with lemon wedges or slices.

Rev. Ken Fleck

Lazy Man's Hors d'Oeuvres

2 (8 oz.) pkg. cream cheese
1 pkg. Wakefield's frozen crab-shrimp mixture, defrosted
1 bottle Hoffman House cocktail sauce
Assorted crackers

Place shrimp-crabmeat mixture over cream cheese and pour cocktail sauce over all ingredients. Serve with assorted crackers.

Rev. Leon R. Wagner

Super Fruit Dip

1 (8 oz.) pkg. cream cheese
1 (8 oz.) jar of Marshmallow Fluff
1 T. lemon, lime, or orange juice
grated rind of 1 lemon, lime, or orange

Soften the cream cheese and blend in the fluff with a mixer. This will be sticky mess at first but will eventually smooth out. Add juice and rind, and put in a covered bowl and refrigerate to blend flavors till ready to serve. Arrange fresh fruit slices (melon, apples, pears, banana chunks) or whole fruits (berries, grapes, etc.) on a platter and serve with dip on the side. Great summer appetizer or dessert.

Rev. Jerry Williams, O. Carm.

Italian Sausage Appetizer

1 lb. of hot Italian sausage
2 lbs. of mild Italian sausage
2 large green peppers
1 med. yellow onion
1 small jalapeno pepper
olive oil
balsamic vinegar
salt
2 garlic cloves, crushed
Crusty Italian bread

Cut up sausage into 1 to 2 inch cubes and cook in large skillet until no longer pink. Set aside. Drain skillet. Lightly coat skillet with olive oil. Slice peppers and onions julienne style and sauté with the garlic cloves until starting to get soft. Salt to taste. Add the cooked sausage and fill skillet with balsamic vinegar. Cover and cook until vegetables are soft. Serve with crusty Italian bread and red wine. Reheats well in the microwave. Also makes a great lunch.

Rev. Dominick J. Grassi

Shoes of the Fisherman

1 (8 oz.) pkg. cream cheese
2 t. chopped onion
1-1/2 c. crab meat, drained and flaked (7-1/2 oz. can)
2 t. milk
1/2 t. horseradish
1/3 c. toasted almonds, slivered
Cocktail rye bread

Combine softened cheese, crabmeat, onion, milk, and horseradish. Mix well until blended. Spoon into 9-inch pie plate or oven proof dish. Sprinkle with almonds. Bake at 375 degrees for 15 minutes. Serve on cocktail rye slices.

Rev. Maurice Kissane

Spinach Dip

1 pkg. frozen spinach cooked, chopped, and drained
1 c. mayonnaise
1 c. sour cream
 pkg. Knorr's leek soup mix
1 bunch (6-8) green onions
dash Tabasco sauce (optional)
1 Holland Dutch Loaf
French bread slices

Mix all ingredients. Chill several hours. Serve in hollowed bread loaf (Holland Dutch Loaf). Place French bread slices around the loaf.

Rev. Edwin Bohula (Capt., CHC, USN, Ret.)

What's for Dinner?

An elderly pastor was invited to dinner at the home of a parishioner.

While the parents were in the kitchen preparing to serve dinner he was left with children at the table. He asked one of the children, "*What are we having for dinner?*"

The first grader spoke up, "*Goat.*"

"Goat?!?" gasped the pastor. "*What makes you think we're having goat for dinner?*"

The child responded, "*I heard Dad tell Mom last night, 'Might as well have the old goat for dinner tomorrow night.*"

Notes

Beverages

Happy Cook, just take a look
To find a secret in this book.
There's something here for old and young
To please the pocket, heart, and tongue.

Irene Hayes
St. George Parish

Aromatic Mexican Coffee

coffee
purified water
ground cinnamon

Use regular coffee maker. Place coffee grounds into filter. Use a small amount of cinnamon powder, sprinkle on top of coffee grounds. Add water. Let the percolating begin! Notice the aroma that the coffee gives off.

Most Rev. Placido Rodriguez, CMF
Bishop of Lubbock

Irish Cream

3 eggs
1/4 t. almond extract
1 can Eagle brand condensed milk
1/2 c. whipping cream
1 c. Whiskey
1-1/2 t. Nestles Quik

Beat eggs in blender, Pour into bowl. Add other ingredients and stir gently, mixing well. Refrigerate and shake before serving over ice.

Rev. Terrence A. McCarthy

Coffee

Mix your regular pot of coffee to your strength and add one cinnamon stick to the pot and let it steep for at least 15 minutes. One stick is good for a couple of pots of coffee. A wonderful treat, simple to make for holidays or special occasions.

VIENNESE

To your favorite coffee add 1/4 c. instant hot chocolate mix and top with whipped cream. Dust with powdered cocoa for a garnish (optional).

LIMITED BY YOUR IMAGINATION COFFEE

Add a shot of your favorite brandy (approx. 2 T.) per cup of coffee, e.g. Chocolate Vandermint, Irish Whisky

Rev. Ken Fleck

Bishop Jakubowski's Holiday Glogg

Into large enamel or porcelain pot (not metal) place:

4 dried prunes
1-2 handfuls seedless raisins
1/2 handful chopped dried dates (optional)
1-2 cinnamon sticks (or more)
8-10 cloves (or more)
8-10 cardamom seeds (or a pinch of powder)
1 orange peel (or more)
some blanched slivered almonds
pinch of nutmeg (or more)
2-3 dried apricots or peaches (optional)
1/2 c. sugar

Cover with water. Add if you like, 1/2 c. rum and/or 1/2 c. high alcoholic spirits. (110-190 proof) Bring to a boil. Then add:

1/5 bottle of burgundy
1/5 bottle of port
1/5 bottle of brandy

Do <u>not</u> boil! Serve hot in mug or Old Fashioned glass.

Most Rev. Thad Jakubowski, D.D.
Auxiliary Bishop of the Archdiocese of Chicago

Daiquiri Punch

1/2 c. light corn syrup
2 c. light rum
2 cans (6 oz. each) frozen daiquiri mix (thawed)
2 bottles carbonated water
ice ring
1 lime, thinly sliced

Mix corn syrup and rum in punch bowl, stirring to blend. Stir in daiquiri mix.

Just before serving, add carbonated water, then carefully slide in ice ring and add lime slices.

Rev. Edwin Bohula (Capt., CHC, USN, Ret.)

Shakin' The Heat Wave

I call this drink the "heat wave" since it is best served when the temperature is hot. Something to cool you down without adding a lot of calories to your diet.

In a blender add:

2 c. water
2/3 c. powdered non-fat dry milk

You can substitute milk of your choosing rather than dry milk. Dry milk allows you to thicken the shake. Blend on low speed. Add flavors of choice at this point:

Some variations are:

- **3 T. cocoa powder**
- **1 t. vanilla extract, or coconut extract, or rum extract, or chocolate extract**
- **1 c. blueberries or 1 medium banana or**
- **1 c. strawberries**

For children's tastes you may wish to use Jell-O crystals for flavoring and variety.

You are only limited by your creativity and imagination and the extracts on hand.

5 packets sugar substitute
2 c. ice cubes (this also thickens the shake)

Frappe with blender until smooth and as thick as you like.

Rev. Ken Fleck

Orange Crush Crush

1 orange
orange juice, prefer 100%, but NOT made from concentrate
ice cubes

Crush 6 or 8 ice cubes into a large tall glass. Peel orange and separate the wedges. Cut each wedge into 3 pieces and mash them in a bowl. Pour orange juice over contents. Fill the glass.

Drink leisurely. If that doesn't pick you up, you need a vacation.

Rev. James E. Flynn

Mash Brew

I have in my possession an old diary that has been passed through many hands since as early as 1914. Several of those hands have left curious jottings. I here share for the first time what, to me, is one of the most curious of all – in an unaltered text that seems to leave a lot of details to the imagination – my Great Grandma O'Neill's recipe for Mash Brew.

10 lbs. rye
10 lbs. cracked corn
30 lbs. sugar
2 lbs. yeast

Put grains in 36 QT. stainless steel stock pot. Cover grains with 5 gal. of water. Let set for 10 days. Skim surface. Add sugar boil well. Allow to cool until warm to touch. Add yeast, stir. Cover with plastic wrap (modern convenience). Allow to fement 14 to 21 days. Sample periodically. When ready bottle in brown beer bottles with crown caps.

Rev. Dennis O'Neill

The Cruise Drink

5 parts orange juice
1 part vodka (2 parts if you're daring)
1 part crème de banana
1/4 part grenadine

Mix, stir, pour over ice, enjoy!

Rev. Rich Homa

Notes

Day Two

Where did I put that glass bowl?

"God said, 'Let there be a vault in the waters to divide the waters in two.' And so it was. God made the vault from the waters under the vault."

Genesis 1:6-7

Soups

Chicken Noodle Soup

Don't throw them chicken bones out along with the back, neck and carcass of a roasted chicken. Make soup! BC (Be Creative!)

Place the chicken parts and/or carcass in a pot with about

8 c. boiling water.
1 medium onion
3 stalks celery
2-4 bullion cubes to heighten the flavor (or you can substitute chicken broth for water in part or whole.)

After the meat has simmered for about 1 hour remove bones from soup and take meat from bones when cool enough to handle. Return meat to the pot. Add onions and celery and bullion cubes one at a time to adjust the flavor intensity.

Add a starch like rice (leftovers are good here)

> or 1 c. uncooked rice,
> or you can add linguine noodles that have been broken,
> or other pasta shapes that suit your taste.

Cook another 20-30 minutes until pasta or rice is done.

Rev. Ken Fleck

Split Pea Soup

In the chill of winter nothing takes the bite out of the weather like homemade soup. This is easy when done in a crock-pot.

4 **c. dry green split peas**
4 **quarts water**
1 **ham bone with some meat on it.**
  (This can be from a dinner a month ago. Just keep it in the freezer.)
1 **large onion, diced (about 2 c.)**
1 **T. Mrs. Dash**
1 **T. liquid smoke**
2 **c. carrots, diced**

This can be done overnight for lunch the next day or in the morning for dinner when using the crock pot.

Clean and pick over split peas to pull out any gravel or discolored peas. Add peas, water, ham bone, and onion to crock pot. Allow to cook on low overnight or for an extended period of time (5 hours or more). To quicken the process use boiling water and turn crock pot to high for 2 to 3 hours. Stir occasionally.

After a few hours of cooking and simmering pull the ham bone out to trim the meat off. (Allow it to cool for about 30 minutes before handling.) You don't have a ham bone? Use smoked sausage or smoked turkey meat.

Return the meat the to soup. Stir to mash the peas. Add the seasonings and liquid smoke. Add carrots 30 minutes before serving–al dente. For softer veggies add earlier in the cooking. Salt and pepper to taste, add milk to thin.

Rev. Ken Fleck

The Combination Connection

(Soup de Jour)

So often we limit ourselves to opening a can of soup and serving what that particular can has to offer. With a little creativity, sharing in God's talents he gave you, you can take the ordinary and make something extraordinary. Here are some examples to get you start - ed:

When I refer to 1 can that means a 10-1/2 oz. can.

- 2 cans low fat or no fat chicken broth, 2 stalks celery, 2 carrots (diced), 1 medium onion, and 1 c. your favorite pasta

- 1 can cream of celery, leftover veggies from the night before, spice with a little chopped onion, add one can milk.

- 1 can cheddar cheese soup, 1 c. florets of broccoli and/or cauli-flower, 1 c. milk.

- 1 can split pea soup, 1 c. diced smoked sausage, 1 small onion diced, dash of liquid smoke, 1 can milk.

- 1 can split pea soup, 1 can cream of tomato soup, 1 can milk or half & half, 1/2 lb. shrimp small to medium size peeled and cleaned, 2 T. dry sherry.

BE CREATIVE!!!

Rev. Ken Fleck

Bean Soup

The crock pot makes soup making so easy. Every kitchen should have one to help us learn how to slow down yet still enjoy good cooking without all the fuss.

2 lbs. your favorite beans—
>   **You can mix and match. BE CREATIVE!!!**

3-1/2 qts. water
1 ham bone
>   **or 1 lb. smoked sausage**
>   **or 2 lbs. smoked turkey wings, legs, etc.**

1 T. liquid smoke
1 medium onion, diced
1 t. seasoned salt
1 t. cayenne pepper
1 bay leaf
1/2 t. freshly ground pepper

Use a large 5 quart crock pot. Recipe can be cut in half if using a 3-1/2 qt. crock pot.

Quick start is to use boiling water over the washed and picked beans in the crock pot with all the seasonings and set on high. Like the split peas this can be done overnight or during the day on low heat and kicked up to high to finish the soup.

After a few hours of cooking in the crock pot remove the ham bone and trim the meat. Return the meat to the soup. Cook until beans are tender. Adjust seasoning to taste. If you don't like it hot, take out the cayenne. You can always kick it up with crushed red pepper or hot sauce.

Rev. Ken Fleck

Fantastic Minestrone Soup

1 c. chopped onion
1 c. chopped celery
1 clove garlic, minced
1/4 c. olive oil
1 (12 oz.) tomato paste
2 cans beef broth
2-1/2 qt. water
2 c. chopped or shredded cabbage
I box frozen peas and carrots
2 t. salt
1/4 t. ground pepper
1/2 t. rosemary
1 can drained kidney beans
1 c. elbow macaroni

Cook onion, celery, and garlic in oil until tender. Stir in tomato paste, broth, water, cabbage, salt, rosemary, pepper, peas, and carrots. Heat to boil. Simmer covered about 1 hour. Stir in beans and macaroni and simmer until tender, about 15 minutes. Cool and Enjoy!

Rev. Edwin Bohula (Capt., CHC, USN, Ret.)

Mushroom Soup

I like the simple but elegant recipes too.

1/2 lb. your favorite mushrooms
   Try experimenting with different mushrooms especially exotic ones. Dry mushrooms have more concentrated flavors.
1 can cream of mushroom soup
1 can milk
1 small onion, diced and sautéed
3 slices bacon

Clean the mushrooms and slice or keep small mushrooms whole. Fry bacon. Remove most of the fat and discard. In the same pan, sauté the onions and mushrooms lightly, 2 to 3 minutes.

In a large sauce pan combine soup, milk, onions and mushrooms. Crumble the bacon and garnish the soup with bacon bits. You can also add some snipped parsley or chives.

Rev. Ken Fleck

French Onion Soup

3 large onions, sliced about 1/4 inch thick
3 T. vegetable oil
4 c. beef broth
3 T. dry sherry
1 t. salt
1/2 t. freshly ground pepper
French bread, sliced thin and toasted
grated Parmesan cheese

In a large, deep skillet sauté the onions over medium low heat until they are caramelized—rich brown in color. Add the beef broth, sherry, and pepper. Bring to a boil. Reduce heat to simmer for about 30 minutes. (You can also use the crock pot and let it cook on low for a long time.

Two ways to serve:

Simple: Pour hot soup into bowls. Top with a toasted round of French bread and sprinkle generously with Parmesan cheese.

Elegant: When ready to serve pour soup into oven safe bowls. Float toasted French bread rounds on the soup, sprinkle with shredded mozzarella. Place under a broiler for 1-2 minutes to lightly brown and bubble the cheese. Serve grated Parmesan on the table as a garnish for your guests to use.

Rev. Ken Fleck

Onion Soup

4 c. water
5 or 6   bouillon beef bouillon cubes
         (Substitute low fat, low sodium, canned beef broth, approx.
         30 oz. for water & bouillon cubes).
1 t. seasoning salt (substitute 1 T. Mrs. Dash)
1/4 t. fresh ground pepper
3 c. onions, sliced thinly and sautéed
3 T. vegetable oil

Place oil and onions in a covered skillet over medium heat for ten minutes. Turn heat to high and while constantly turning the onions continue sautéing until dark brown (about 12 minutes.)

Add onions to beef broth and simmer on low for 30 minutes or in a crock pot (low) for up to 2 hours to improve flavor.

Serving suggestions:

Place servings in oven proof bowls. Float a piece of dry French bread on top of each bowl of soup and top with Swiss cheese or mozzarella. Place bowls on a cookie sheet under a broiler for approx. 2 minutes until cheese starts to turn brown. Serves 6.

Rev. Ken Fleck

Potato Soup

If you ever wondered what to do with leftover mashed pota-toes, here's one solution. (Leftover potatoes can be used in potato pancakes, potato patties served with eggs in the morning or as a side to the main dinner.)

2 T. extra virgin olive oil
1 med. onion, diced
1 t. salt
1 t. Mrs. Dash
1/2 t. celery salt
fresh ground pepper to taste
4 c. milk
3 to 4 c. leftover mashed potatoes
    or 1-1/2 c. instant mashed potatoes
    or 3 baked leftover potatoes
    or 3 fresh potatoes, peeled, eyes removed, and grated.

In a large deep skillet add olive oil. Sauté the onion until tender, not brown. Add seasonings, milk and potatoes. Continue cooking until smooth. Mashed potatoes and instant will cook quickly. Baked potatoes (skinned) and fresh potatoes will take longer.

After cooking for about 20 minutes place soup in a food processor or blender and puree until a smooth consistency is reached. It will be the consistency of a thin pancake batter.

Garnish with sprigs of parsley, snipped chives and/or a dash or paprika.

Rev. Ken Fleck

Robert's Ramen Soup Combos

It seems obvious, but sometimes the obvious needs to be stated to uncover creativity. Creative cooking is not defined by developing something "completely different" but by taking what you have and coming up with a combination you like.

Shrimp Ramen Soup:

In a 10-inch saucepan sauté any or all of the following:

3 T. vegetable oil
1/2 c. celery, diced
1/2 c. onion, chopped
1/2 c. mushrooms, sliced

Low fat version, skip the oil and proceed to next step.
Low sodium version, use only half seasoning packet, and add 2 t. low sodium, mushroom flavored soy sauce.

To this follow Ramen package directions. Break up noodles in package. Add two cups water to veggies. Bring to a boil. Add noodles. Add twenty medium-sized, frozen, shrimp and seasoning packet. Cover for 3 to 4 minutes. Serves 2 with crackers or bread and salad. A light and easy meal.

Blue Collar Beef Ramen:

10-inch saucepan as before. Sauté any or all of the following:

1/2 c. green pepper

1/2 c. onion, chopped

1/2 lb. raw beef, cubed or leftover beef, diced.

Add one can (12 oz.) beer. *(This is obviously not for the kids.)* Break up the noodles in the package. Add to pan. Add seasoning to taste. Cut back on the sodium by substituting other flavors, low sodium soy sauces, garlic, or curry or try these other versions.

Hunan Version: Add crushed 1/2 red pepper or a hot chili diced and sautéed with the onion and green pepper to taste.

Western Version: Add 1 T. chili powder to the basic seasoning.

Rev. Ken Fleck

Chicken Ramen

You know the basics by now. Sauté any or all in 3 T. vegetable oil:

1/2 c. onion
1/2 c. diced celery
1/2 c. peanuts or cashews
1/2 lb. white chicken meat cubed or leftovers

Add the water, noodles, and 1-2 T. curry powder to taste with seasoning packet.

Gold Coast Version

Substitute 1/2 can mushroom soup for 1 c. water, 1 jigger (2-3 oz.) dry sherry, and 1/2 lb. your favorite mushroom (try a new one, be wild!) Skip the other veggies.

Different veggies combined with different nuts and creamed soups give you an unlimited variety. Don't be afraid to experiment.

Ramen soups are a wonderful way to deal with leftover veggies, meat, etc. in a creative way that has the family or guests amazed at your creativity.

Rev. Ken Fleck

Zesty Tomato Soup

6 tomatoes, sliced fine
1 large onion, diced
1/4 head of cabbage, cut up
4 stocks of celery, diced
4 carrots, diced
1 large can of chicken broth
3 cloves garlic, crushed
dash nutmeg, to taste
dash sugar, to taste
dash all spice, to taste
curry powder, to taste
cloves, to taste

Mix tomatoes, onions, cabbage, celery, carrots, and crushed garlic in chicken broth. Simmer until vegetables are tender; then add the rest of the ingredients to taste.

Br. Leonard M. Lawrence, OFM

Cajun Gumbo

4   slices bacon
4   T. flour
4   ribs of celery, chopped
2   small green peppers
1   lb. okra, sliced
2   bunches green onions, chopped
1/2 c. green tops, chopped
1   large onion, chopped
1   1 lb. can tomatoes with liquid
    salt and pepper to taste
1   quart shrimp, peeled and deveined
1   quart crab meat
12 crab shells and bodies
1   T. Gumbo Filé
lots of rice

Fry bacon in skillet; drain slices. Add flour to bacon drippings; brown. Add celery, pepper, okra, and onions; stir and cook 15 minutes. Add tomatoes and simmer for 10 minutes. Add contents to large pot. Add 2 tomato cans of water, and bring to a boil. Season with salt and pepper (hot sauce if desired). Add shrimp, crab meat, shells, and bodies. Add green onions and tops; simmer for at least 2 hours. Add gumbo filé 30 minutes before serving. Serve over rice. Serves 12 or 4 hungry priests.

Rev. Phillip Kiley, in memory of Rev. Vic Stewart

Southwest Chicken Soup

1 c. chopped onion
1/2 c. chopped celery
1 T. olive oil
6 c. chicken stock
4 chicken breast halves
1 can (4 oz.) chopped green chilis
1/2 c. brown rice
1 pkg. (10 oz.) frozen cut corn
1 t. cumin
1 T. chili powder
2 T. picante sauce
1 can (15-1/2 oz.) diced tomatoes

In a soup pot sauce onions and celery in oil until soft. Add chicken stock, chicken pieces, and brown rice. Bring mixture to a boil. Reduce heat, cover, and simmer until chicken is tender, 20 to 30 minutes.

Remove chicken and set aside to cool. Continue simmering for 15 minutes. Remove chicken from the bone and add back to the stock with the remaining ingredients. Heat through, adjust seasonings.

Rev. Quinn R. Conners, O. Carm.

Vatican Fried Chicken

During a Papal audience, a business man approached the Pope and made this offer: Change the last line of the Lord's prayer from "Give us this day our daily bread." to "Give us this day our daily chicken," and Kentucky Fried Chicken will donate $10,000,000 to Catholic charities. The Pope declined.

Two weeks later, the man approached the Pope again—this time with a $50,000,000 offer. Again, the Pope declined. A month later, the man upped the price to $100,000,000, and this time the Pope accepted. At a meeting of the Cardinals, the Pope announced his decision in the good news/bad news format. "The good news is: We have $100,000,000 for charities. The bad news: We lost the Wonder Bread account.

Notes

Salads

Becky's Sunflower Surprise

3/4 c. fat free cottage cheese
1/2 c. crushed pineapple
1 med. banana
1 maraschino cherry, stem removed

Spread the cottage cheese evenly in the bottom of a cereal bowl. Place the cherry in the middle of the cheese. On top of the cherry place the pineapple in a mound. Cut the banana into cartwheels and place around the pineapple.

Serves 1 with a minimum of calories and maximum of taste.

Rev. Ken Fleck

Broccoli Raisin Salad

1 large head of broccoli, chopped
1/2 onion, chopped
1 lb. bacon, fried crisp and crumbled
1 c. raisins
<u>Dressing</u>
Combine and chill:
    1 c. mayonnaise
    1/4 c. vinegar
    1/4 c. sugar
    powdered garlic to taste

Combine vegetables in a bowl. Approximately 20 minutes prior to serving, add bacon and dressing. Toss.

Rev. Terrence A. McCarthy by Elizabeth A. Ryan

Judy's Dump Salad

1 6 oz. pkg. lime Jell-O
1 large carton small curd cottage cheese
1 20 oz. can crushed pineapple, drained well
1 c. chopped nuts
1 large container Cool Whip

Leaving the Jell-O powder dry, add all ingredients in order, one at a time and mix well between additions. Refrigerate several hours before serving, and stir well before serving.

Rev. Jerry Williams, O. Carm.

Caesar Salad

2 T. salad oil
1 clove garlic
2 c. bread cubes
1 large head of romaine lettuce
1 large head of head lettuce
1/4 c. grated Parmesan cheese
1/4 c. crumbled bleu cheese
6 or 8 anchovy fillets, chopped
1/2 c. salad oil
1/4 c. lemon juice
dash pepper
3/4 t. salt
1/4 t. dry mustard
1 egg, hard boiled

In a small skillet add 2 T. salad oil and the peeled and split garlic clove and sauté over a low heat until the garlic is yellow, not brown. Remove the garlic from the oil. Add the bread cubes to the oil and heat, stirring occasionally, until lightly browned. Remove from skillet and set aside to cool.

Tear crisp, chilled romaine and head lettuce into bite size pieces and arrange them in a salad bowl. Sprinkle with cheeses and anchovy bits. Combine the 1/2 c. salad oil, lemon juice, pepper, salt, and dry mustard. Whisk or shake to blend. Pour over the greens and toss lightly to coat. Break the egg into the greens and toss lightly until the egg particles disappear. Add browned bread cubes and toss. Serve at once. Serves 6.

Rev. Dennis O'Neill

Eileen's Patriotism

3/4 c. Fat Free cottage cheese
1/2 c. fresh strawberries
1/2 c. fresh blueberries

Spread the cottage cheese evenly in the bottom of a cereal bowl. Place the blueberries in the middle of the cheese in a mound. Cut the strawberries in half lengthwise and place around the blueberry mound.

Serves 1 with a minimum of calories and maximum of taste.

Rev. Ken Fleck

Cool as a Cucumber Salad Variations

I usually grow my own cucumbers on chain link fences at my different assignments. Here are recipes for cool salads on the hot days of summer.

4 medium size cucumbers
3-4 t. salt
1 c. white vinegar
2-3 T. sugar
Fresh ground pepper

Peel the skin from the cucumbers. Slice very thinly, such that they are flimsy. Let stand in a bowl at room temperature for 1-2 hours. Squeeze the water out of them. They can also be placed in a colander with a plate on them and a heavy object on the plate to help in this process.

Combine in a bowl the vinegar, salt, sugar and pepper. Pour over the cucumbers. Cover and refrigerate for 2 hours or overnight. Drain the liquid before serving.

Two alternate dressings for thinly sliced cucumbers:
  2 c. sour half and half or sour cream
  1 t. dry dill weed or 1 T. fresh dill weed.
  1 t. salt
  Fresh ground pepper.

Mix all ingredients together. Lightly toss with cucumbers. Refrigerate for 2 hours.

For more zest add the following ingredients to this second dressing.
  1-2 t. minced fresh garlic
  2 T. vegetable oil
  2 t. sugar
  1 t. white vinegar

Garnish salad before serving with any of the following:
  - snipped chives
  - parsley
  - dill weed
  - sprinkle of sweet paprika

Rev. Ken Fleck

Calico Coleslaw

2 c. green cabbage, shredded
2 c. red cabbage, shredded
1 t. dried chives
1 c. low fat plain yogurt or sour cream
3 T. vinegar
2 T. sugar
1 t. salt

Toss shredded cabbage together with chives. Combine remaining ingredients to make dressing. Mix well with cabbage mixture.

Yields 6 servings.

Rev. Joseph A. Lawler

Hot Chicken Salad

2 c. chopped cooked chicken or turkey
2 c. chopped celery
1/2 t. salt
2 t. chopped green onions
1 c. mayonnaise
2 T. lemon juice
1 c. grated cheddar cheese
1 c. seasoned breadcrumbs (croutons)
paprika

Mix all ingredients except croutons and paprika the night before and refrigerate. When ready to bake, mix in the croutons, pile into a casserole dish and sprinkle with paprika and a little more cheese. Bake at 350 degrees for 20 minutes. Makes 6 servings.

Rev. Jerry Williams, O. Carm.

German Potato Salad

Whenever I visit my relatives in Austria a favorite dish of mine is their potato salads. They have a butter yellow potato that has a creamy, wonderful taste in all its forms.

2-3 lbs. potatoes (6-8 medium sized)
6 slices bacon
1 c. onion, chopped
2 T. flour
2 T. sugar
2 t. salt
1 t. celery seed
freshly ground pepper
1 c. water
1/2 c. vinegar

Peel potatoes. Remove skin and eyes. Cut into quarters and place in a large saucepan. Cover with water and bring to a boil. Cover and cook for approximately 30 minutes until fork tender. Drain and set aside.

In a large skillet fry bacon until crisp. Drain fat saving about 1/4 c. in the pan. Sauté the onion until tender. Stir in flour, sugar, salt, celery seed, and pepper to taste. Add water and vinegar. Lower the heat and continue cooking until thick and bubbly. Slice potatoes thinly and add to the sauce with the bacon crumbled. Stir gently to coat and heat for another two minutes.

Can be garnished with hard-boiled eggs and additional bacon crumbled on top.

Rev. Ken Fleck

No Jell-O Jell-O Mold - Pink Stuff

1 can (8 oz.) Solo brand cherry or strawberry pie filling
1 can (20 oz.) crushed pineapple with juice
1 can (12 fl. oz.)Eagle brand milk
1 carton (9 oz.) Cool Whip
1 c. chopped nuts

Mix all together and pour into 9x13 inch casserole dish. Freeze overnight covered with foil or Saran Wrap. Remove from freezer 1 hour before serving.

Rev. Jerry Williams, O. Carm.

Egg Salad for 4

4 hard-boiled eggs
4 tomatoes
1 head of lettuce
Dressing:
    1 t. salt
    2 T. Worcestershire sauce
    4 T. olive oil
    4 T. vinegar

Chop whites of eggs small. Put yolks through sieve. Chop tomatoes fine. Make a mound of salt in a jar. Pour Worcestershire sauce around it. Add 4 T. of olive oil and 4 T. of vinegar. Shake well.

Put lettuce in salad bowls. Top with tomatoes, then egg whites and lastly egg yolks. Pour dressing over it and serve.

Msgr. Francis J. McElligott

Waldorf Salad

Whenever using fresh fruit that will be cut in a recipe, if it will not be served and eaten immediately, use a little lemon juice to prevent oxida - tion (when the fruit turns brown).

4 c. apples, cored and diced (leave the skin on)
1 T. lemon juice
1/2 c. celery, chopped
1 c. seedless grapes
1/2 c. walnuts, chopped
1/2 c. mayonnaise or salad dressing
1/2 c. Cool Whip
1 t. lemon juice

In a large bowl toss apples lightly with 1 T. lemon juice to coat. Add celery, grapes, and walnuts. In a small bowl mix the mayo, Cool Whip and 1 t. lemon juice. Combine the mixture into the large bowl with the other ingredients and gently toss to coat.

Garnish by serving on crisp lettuce leaves, with a maraschino cherry on top and a few powdered sugar coated grapes on the side.

Rev. Ken Fleck

Lemon Greek Salad

1 medium cucumber, unpeeled
2 c. spinach, bite-sized pieces
2 c. Boston lettuce, bite-sized pieces
1/4 c. feta cheese, crumbled
2 T. sliced green onions with tops
10 pitted ripe olives
1 medium tomato, cut into thin wedges
lemon and mustard dressing (below)

Score cucumber by running tines of fork lengthwise down the sides, then slice. Toss cucumber and remaining ingredients.

Lemon and Mustard Dressing

2 T. lemon juice
1 T. olive or vegetable oil
1 t. sugar
1 t. Dijon mustard
1/8 t. pepper

Shake all ingredients in a tightly closed container. Serves 4.

Br. Robert Fandel, OSM

Day Three

Hmmmmmm. Too much water.

"God said, 'Let the waters under heaven come together into a single mass, and let dry land appear.' And so it was. God called the dry land 'earth' and the mass of waters 'seas', and God saw that it was good."

Genesis 1:9-10

Sauces

Blender Pesto Sauce

2 c. fresh basil leaves
1/2 c. olive oil
2 T. pine nuts
2 cloves garlic, crushed
1 t. salt
1/2 c. Parmesan cheese, freshly grated
2 T. Romano cheese, freshly grated
3 T. butter, softened

Put basil, oil, pine nuts, garlic, and salt in blender and mix at high speed. Stop from time to time to scrape sides and blend. When evenly blended, pour into bowl and beat in 2 cheeses by hand. When they are blended, add the butter. Before spooning pesto over pasta, add 1 T. of the hot water in which the pasta has boiled. *Do not crush the basil. Gently tear larger leaves before the blending.*

This can be frozen, but only the ingredients blended in the blender, not the cheeses or butter.

Rev. Robert Hutmacher, OFM

Caesar Salad Dressing

1/2 c. olive oil
2 crushed garlic cloves
1/2 t. Worcestershire sauce
1/4 t. sugar
1/4 t. mustard powder
1/4 t. salt
1/4 t. pepper
1/4 c. Parmesan cheese
2 T. lemon juice
1 t. anchovy paste

Mix all together well and shake before pouring over greens. Add bacon bits, mushrooms, onion rings, and croutons if desired.

Rev. Jerry Williams, O. Carm.

Cheese Sauce
(For vegetables or fish)

1 c. mayonnaise or Miracle Whip
1 c. shredded cheese
   (I prefer blends that are readily available in 8 oz. packages.)
1/2 c. milk

Combine all ingredients in a saucepan over low heat until blended, stirring constantly.
Garnish Choices to add flair and flavor:
— red, green, or orange sweet bell peppers, diced or sliced
— fresh sliced mushrooms
—dash of paprika and fresh chopped parsley

Rev. Ken Fleck

Polka's Steak Marinade

1 bottle soy sauce
dry Vermouth, equal to the amount of soy sauce
2 minced garlic cloves
1 T. powdered ginger
2 T. sugar

Place all ingredients in a jar and shake well till blended. This is a superb marinade for steaks or lamb chops for the grill.

Rev. Jerry Williams, O. Carm.

Fresh Tomato Dressing

3 T. good olive oil
1 T. red wine vinegar
1 T. fresh lime juice
1 t. garlic powder
salt to taste
Tabasco sauce to taste

Shake together in a salad cruet and pour over fresh, sliced tomatoes. Garnish with fresh parsley or oregano.

Rev. Jerry Williams, O. Carm.

Hot Tomato & Vegetable Sauce
(low sodium, low cholesterol)

1 can (15 oz.) special tomato sauce (with vegetable bits)
1 can (8 oz.) regular tomato sauce
4 sweet gherkin pickles, finely chopped
6 dashes hot pepper sauce
1 t. thyme
1 t. ground pepper
1/2 lb. mushrooms, sliced
8 green onions, finely chopped
3 cloves garlic, finely chopped
2 T. olive oil
1/4 c. parsley, chopped

Simmer tomato sauces, pickles, hot sauce, thyme, and pepper in saucepan. Sauté mushrooms, onions and garlic in olive oil; continue until water is all cooked off. Mix with tomato sauce mixture. Simmer 5 minutes more. Add chopped parsley and serve. Use with ground meat dishes-meatloaf, hamburgers, stuffed peppers, sloppy Joes.

Rev. William A. Schumacher

Ma Keating's Pantry Secrets
Salad Dressing All'Italiana

1 c. Wesson oil or olive oil
1/3 c. wine vinegar
1/2 t. liquid sweetener or equivalent
1 t. ground mustard
1 t. celery seed
1/2 t. salt
1/4 t. pepper
1 small onion or 1 clove garlic

Into a bottle container, pour the mustard, celery seed, salt, and pepper. Add vinegar and shake well. Add oil and sweetener; shake again. Drop onion or garlic clove into container and shake again. Keep refrigerated.

Most Rev. John R. Keating
Bishop of Arlington

Just Like Mom's (Almost) Tomato Sauce

3 bottles any quality tomato sauce
1 carrot
1 onion
1 c. dry red wine
1 clove garlic
2 T. sugar

Bring sauce to boil with carrot, onion and garlic placed in whole. Add wine and sugar and let simmer in low heat for 1/2 hour to an hour.

Guaranteed to taste homemade all the way!

Rev. Dominic J. Grassi

Crabmeat Sauce for Pasta

1 c. heavy cream (whipping cream)
8 oz. crabmeat, lump or flaked
1/4 c. fresh parsley, chopped
1 t. dry basil

In a large deep skillet gently warm the cream. When warm add the crabmeat and basil. Prepare your favorite pasta al dente. Drain. Add to the skillet. Toss to evenly coat the pasta. Let rest 5 minutes before serving. Garnish with the fresh parsley.

Rev. Ken Fleck

Raisin Rum Sauce

2 T. butter
1 c. sugar
2 T. rum
1/2 c. golden or dark raisins

Mix all ingredients in a small sauce pan and heat gently until sugar is dissolved. May be thinned with more rum.

Rev. Ken Fleck

Mushroom-Bacon (Ham) Sauce

1-1/4 c. (1-1/2 oz.) dried mushroom
(porcini or other wild mushroom)
2 c. boiling water
1/2 c. crumbled bacon or ham
1 shallot or small onion, minced
2 T. extra virgin olive oil
freshly ground pepper
1 c. heavy cream (whipping cream)
nutmeg to taste

In a small bowl combine the mushrooms and boiling water. Soak the mushrooms for at least 30 minutes or more. You may also do this overnight. Squeeze as much water from the mushrooms. Rinse under fresh water. Take the reserve liquid and strain through cheesecloth.

In a large deep skillet over a medium heat add the oil, onion, and bacon or ham, sauté until transparent, 3 to 4 minutes. Add the mushrooms that have been coarsely chopped, cook for 4 minutes more. Add cream and nutmeg to taste. Cook for a couple of minutes and add the reserve mushroom liquid. Cook for 25 minutes stirring occasionally.

Cook your favorite pasta al dente. Add to the skillet. Toss to coat evenly. Let rest 5 minutes. Serve.

Rev. Ken Fleck

Mom Rocker's Tomato Gravy

1 large or 2 small tomatoes
1/2 t. onion, finely chopped
1/4 c. bacon drippings
1/2 t. baking soda
1/3 c. flour
milk

Peel and chop tomatoes. Finely chop 1/2 t. onion. Sauté tomato and onion in 1/4 c. bacon drippings in a black skillet. When tender add 1/2 t. baking soda, 1/3 c. flour, and enough milk to thicken to desired consistency. Serve over homemade bread, toast or biscuits.

Rev. Jerry Williams, O. Carm.

Breads

A recipe is fun to make,
Bread or biscuit, tart or cake!
Each one gives glory, Lord, to You
And we enjoy such blessings, too!

Irene Hayes
St. George Parish

Breadmaking 101

One of the larger flour producers had a jingle that went, *"Nothin' says lovin', like somethin' from the oven."* It is so true that the aroma of fresh baked bread fills a house and transforms it into a home where you not only hear but feel *"Welcome"*.

Many cooks are turned off by the fact that it takes time to prepare and bake bread. The fact that so many bread machines have flooded the market is no wonder. You can now have the goodness of fresh, homemade bread, but without all the fussing and bother.

I still prefer the old-fashioned way. It allows me a certain creative thinking time to myself, and if I am with others, I can share in the art of conversation and ideas. Baking bread is a wonderful, creative time. I hope these recipes help you get started and lead you to enjoy and share many happy memories in the future.

Yeast is the active ingredient that makes bread rise and also gives the kitchen that wonderful fragrance. It is rare that recipes call for cakes of yeast. If you have an old recipe that does, a conversion for dry yeast is 2-1/2 t. dry equals one cake (3/5 oz.) of compressed yeast. If you happen to buy yeast in jars and bake a lot, 2-1/2 t. equals one packet of dry yeast.

Gluten is the "Sticky stuff" of flour. It is the portion of regular flour that traps the gas produced by yeast and binds bread together. Recipes that call for oat, rye or whole wheat always use some regular flour to help boost the gluten in the recipe, as these other flours do not have enough gluten on their own.

Oils and Fats are also important in making bread. They not only add flavor but also give bread a softer texture.

Sugars help the bread to rise as they feed the yeast.

Temperature is important for yeast. Too hot and you kill the yeast. Too cold and it will not grow. The normal temperature for liquids used in yeast recipes is 105 to 115 degrees. Since your body temperature is 98.6 degrees, the liquid you put your yeast into should feel warm, not hot, to your touch.

Kneading is the means by which flour is mixed into dough. I prefer a large bowl, which limits the flour that gets around the kitchen. Many cooks use a cleaned counter liberally sprinkled with flour as a breadboard. You knead dough by pushing on the dough with the heel of your hand, folding it over toward you, give it a quarter turn and repeat. This is done until the dough no longer sticks to your hands and develops a smooth, elastic texture.

Baking is done so that heat evenly travels around the bread. Usually this means placing the oven rack on the second level from the bottom. This will place the bread, in loaves or pans in the center of the oven and give the most even baking.

Cooling bread is as important as baking it. Remove from the pans immediately and place on a cooling rack away from a draft. The bread will continue to bake and needs to rest for 10 to 15 minutes before cutting. Taking it out of the pan prevents moisture from collecting on the bottom of the bread inside the pan.

Crusts come in many different varieties. To soften a crust after baking, brush lightly with butter or margarine or olive oil and cover with a towel for a few minutes. Those hard crusted Italian and French breads we all love are created in special ovens bakeries have that atomize water while the bread is baking. Just as water and flour gave us paste for school projects, so too, adding moisture as the bread is baking gives just enough to harden the outside for that crusty crispness with the heavenly soft bread hidden within. You can imitate this process by placing a pan of water on the floor of the oven as you bake your bread.

Rev. Ken Fleck

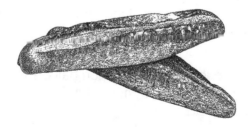

Dinner Rolls

1 pkg. (2-1/2 t.) active dry yeast
1/2 c. warm water
1-1/2 c. warm milk
1/2 c. butter or margarine
1/2 c. sugar
1 t. salt
2 eggs
6 to 7 c. flour

Warm the milk and butter in a saucepan or in a microwave. In a separate bowl mix yeast, a pinch of sugar and the warm water to start the yeast growing.

In a large bowl combine warm milk/butter, sugar, salt, and eggs. Stir in 2 c. flour. Beat until smooth. Continue adding flour until it can be handled easily outside of bowl.

Place dough on a lightly floured breadboard or a clean countertop. Knead with remaining flour until smooth and elastic, about 5 to 10 minutes. Place in a greased bowl and allow to double in size, about 1 to 1-1/2 hours. Dough is ready when it retains an impression when poked. Punch down and divide into four parts.

Rev. Ken Fleck

Variations Of Dinner Rolls

Crescents:

Roll dough into a circle about 12 inches in diameter. Brush the dough with melted butter or margarine. With a pizza wheel cut the dough into wedges, about 12. Roll up beginning at outer edge toward the point. Place rolled up crescents on a lightly greased baking sheet with the point tucked under and give it a crescent curve. Brush with butter.

Cloverleafs:

Take a portion of the dough. Roll into 1 inch balls. Place three dough balls into the greased compartment of a muffin tin.

Parker House:

Roll a portion of the dough into a rectangle about 9x12 inches, brush with butter, cut into 4-inch strips. With the handle of a wooden spoon make an impression in the center of each strip lengthwise. Fold over this crease, cut into 2-inch wide strips and place in a greased baking pan side by side.

Continued on next page

Variations Of Dinner Rolls (Cont'd)

Pan Rolls:

Roll dough into the same rectangle 9x12 inches and place in a similar sized pan. Cut through with a knife or pizza wheel.

Bake at 400 degrees in a preheated oven for 15 to 20 minutes.

Rev. Ken Fleck

Cranberry-Orange Bread

2 c. flour
2 t. baking powder
1/2 t. baking soda
1/2 t. salt
1/3 c. vegetable shortening
2/3 c. sugar
1/2 c. milk
1/3 c. orange juice concentrate
**   or 3 T. grated orange rind**
1 c. cranberries, chopped

Sift flour, baking power, baking soda, and salt twice. Set aside.

In a mixer cream sugar and shortening. Add eggs and mix well. Scrape bowl regularly to blend ingredients. Add milk and orange juice concentrate. (In lieu of milk and o.j. concentrate you can simply add 1 c. orange juice.)

Stir in sifted mixture. (If you like nuts in your bread you can add 1/2 c. chopped pecans or walnuts—optional.)

Bake in a preheated oven at 350 degrees for 50 to 60 minutes or until a toothpick inserted near the center comes out clean. Cool 15 minutes in pan before removing to a cooling rack. Cuts more easily when cooled completely.

Variations:

Substitute golden raisins or chopped dried apricots. If they are a little dry pour boiling water over them or overnight tie in a plastic bag with a few tablespoons of brandy.

Rev. Ken Fleck

Pizzas Galore

Biscuit (p.60) or pizza dough (p. 270) recipe rolled 1/4-inch thick to fit a cast iron skillet or other oven-proof skillet that will fit in the oven.

Add ingredients for a variety of different and intriguing combinations.

A pizza is an open face sandwich. If you view pizzas in this simple form you overcome your fear of making a bad pizza. The fun and creativity are enhanced when those sharing the pizza help put it together. Assemble all your toppings first since the pizza cooks quickly. Heat the skillet(s) on the oven range. Preheat the oven to 500 degrees.

Philadelphia Pan Pizza

Thinly slice leftover steak or steak cooked to your preference. Cut onions and green peppers into large pieces (postage stamp size). Shred or thinly slice mozzarella. Place dough in heated pan and cook on top of stove for two minutes. Flip bread over in pan, top with meat, veggies, and cheese. Place in preheated oven for 5 to 7 minutes.

Vegetarian Variations

Remove core & seeds from green, red, and yellow peppers and slice into thin rings. Thinly slice tomatoes. Thinly slice mushrooms. Prepare the dough as in recipe above. Assemble first with tomatoes, then peppers, onions, mushrooms. Drizzle lightly with extra virgin olive oil. Top with shredded three-cheese combination. Bake in preheated oven for 5 to 7 minutes.

Tex-Mex Express

Your barbecue sauce. Slice leftover chicken or cooked chicken breasts into strips. Slice green peppers into narrow strips. Slice onions into strips. Shred or thinly slice hot pepper cheese or Jalapeno cheese. Prepare your dough in skillet as in basic recipe above. Add your favorite barbecue sauce, meat, green pepper, and onions, top with cheese. To increase the zip, sprinkle with chili powder or crushed red pepper. (It'll make your head sweat!) Bake in preheated oven 5 to 7 minutes.

A Taste Of Italy

Thinly slice your favorite mushrooms. Shred or thinly slice gorgonzola cheese. Prepare your dough in skillet as in recipe on previous page. Lightly brush your pizza dough with extra virgin olive oil. Place the mushrooms on the dough. Top with cheese. Bake in preheated oven for 5 to 7 minutes.

Continued on next page

Pizzas Galore (Cont'd.)

Orient Express

In the microwave thaw a package (8 to 10 oz.). of frozen Oriental veggies. Drain off excess water. To the veggies add 2 t. favorite soy sauce. Toss to coat evenly. Prepare your dough in skillet as in recipe on previous page.   Place veggies evenly on dough. Top with your favorite cheese. Bake in preheated oven for 5 to 7 minutes.

Rev. Ken Fleck

Banana Nut Bread

This is best made with those bananas that look horribly dark brown to black. They are still good. I even look for bananas marked down in the grocery store that start turning. They are excellent for this bread. When the skin starts turning brown the sugar in the skin is being drawn into the fruit.

2 c. flour
2 t. baking powder
1/2 t. baking soda
1/2 t. salt
1/3 c. vegetable shortening
1/2 c. sugar
2 eggs
2 t. milk
2 medium ripe bananas (about 1 c.), mashed
1/2 c. nuts, chopped (optional)

Sift flour, baking powder, baking soda, and salt twice and set aside.

In a mixer bowl cream shortening and sugar. Scrape the sides of the bowl to keep ingredients blending. Add eggs and milk. Add bananas. Stir in sifted ingredients. Add nuts and mix until well blended either by hand or in the mixer.

Pour batter into a lightly greased 8x4x2 inch bread pan. Bake in a preheated oven at 350 degrees for 60 to 65 minutes or until a toothpick inserted in the center comes out clean. Allow to cool and settle in the pan for 15 minutes before removing to a cooling rack. Slices easier when completely cool. Good luck in resisting the urge.

Rev. Ken Fleck

Batter Bread

7-1/2 c. whole wheat flour
2 pkg. dry yeast
1 c. lukewarm water
1 t. honey
1 T. molasses
1 c. warm water
1 T. salt
2 c. (approximately) warm water

Place whole wheat flour in large bowl and set in oven at 140 degrees for 20 minutes to warm flour and bowl. Dissolve yeast in 1 c. lukewarm water and add honey and stir. Let set until flour is ready. Mix molasses with 1 c. warm water. When flour and bowl are warm, pour molasses mixture into yeast mixture and mix well, then add to flour. Add salt. Mix in enough water to make a very sticky dough (about 2 c., but you may need up to 1/2 c. more, depending on what the flour absorbs) No kneading involved. Oil 2 bread pans and put half of mixture into each pan. Let rise 1 hour. Sometimes bread rises in 1/2 hour. Make sure bread rises just short of top of pan.

Meanwhile, preheat oven to 400 degrees. When batter has risen to top of pan, put in oven. Bake for 40 minutes. Cool on racks for 10 minutes. Remove loaves from pans. If bottom is not quite done, put back in oven for 10 to 15 minutes.

Rev. Charles Fanelli

Beer Bread - I

3 c. self-rising flour
3 T. sugar
1 can beer, room temperature
2 eggs

Mix all ingredients and let stand for a few minutes. Pour into a greased loaf pan. Bake at 350 degrees for 60 to 70 minutes. Remove to a cooling rack to cool completely.

Rev. Ken Fleck

Beer Bread - II

2-1/2 c. self-rising flour
　　(or add 2 T. baking powder to regular flour and sift together.)
3 T. sugar
1/2 t. salt
1 can beer

Mix all ingredients together in a large bowl. Grease one bread pan. Allow to rest and rise for 15 minutes. Place in a preheated oven at 350 degrees for 50 minutes.

This bread does not rise high and is dense.

Rev. Ken Fleck

Aunt Minnie's Ginger Bread

Origin: County Clare, Ireland-Circa 1810

2 t. baking soda
1 c. buttermilk
1 c. dark molasses
1/2 c. butter or margarine
1 c. sugar
1 egg
1 t. ginger
1 t. cinnamon
1 t. ground cloves
3 c. all-purpose flour

Mix baking soda and buttermilk. Add molasses.

Melt shortening and add sugar and egg. Add to baking soda and buttermilk. Add spices. Sift flour into mixture. Mix until smooth.

Pour into well-greased 9x13x2 inch pan. Bake at 350 degrees for 35 to 40 minutes. Cake is done when toothpick comes out clean. Cool in pan.

This tasty ginger bread can be served warm with butter. Also delicious frosted with commercial frosting such as Betty Crocker Creamy Vanilla or cream cheese frosting.

Rev. Gene Burns' Kitchen

Short Bread

1 lb. butter
1 c. sugar
4 c. flour

Whip butter till creamy—the longer the better. Add sugar gradually and it becomes very fluffy. Blend in flour, press into a cookie sheet and chill one hour.

Put in a cold oven and bake for 1 hour at 250 degrees.

Rev. Jerry Williams, O. Carm.

Biscuits

2 c. flour
3 t. baking powder
1 t. salt
1/4 c. vegetable shortening
3/4 c. milk

Preheat oven to 450 degrees.

Sift together flour, baking powder and salt. Place in a large howl. Cut in the shortening with two knives, fork or a pastry cutter until it resembles cornmeal or small sized peas. Stir in the milk. Dough should be soft and pliable, not sticky. If it is sticky add a little more flour. If it is too dry, add a little more milk.

Remove the dough from the bowl onto a floured waxed paper or pastry cloth. Knead only to mix the dough to an even texture, a little less than a minute. Too much mixing will make your biscuits tougher.

Roll about 1/2 inch thick, about the thickness of your little finger. Using a biscuit cutter or glass that has been floured cut the dough. Place on an ungreased baking sheet. Bake at 450 degrees for 10 to 12 minutes.

Play God, Be Creative.

Biscuits, like pizza and most bread recipes are limited only by your creative urges and imagination.

Additions to your biscuits might include:

Bacon, shredded cheese, different herbs, garlic, diced onions, seeds, etc.

Continued on next page

Biscuits (Cont'd.)

Soup To Desserts

Biscuits make a wonderful compliment to soups, salads, dinners, etc. But biscuits are useful in many other creative ways:

At breakfast as the underside of eggs benedict.

As a base for strawberry shortcake.

At dinner as a base with your favorite creamed soup and a meat ingredient:

> Chicken breast meat and cream of celery soup.
>
> Smoked salmon and cream of mushroom or shrimp bisque.
>
> Chipped beef or leftover beef and cream of onion soup.

You get the idea. Be creative.

The same dough can be used in making soup and dropping into the broth as it is cooking and makes dumplings, the way grandma used to make soup.

Easier methods for biscuits are found on boxes of packaged biscuit mixes and should be a regular part of any cook's menu. It is also an easy way to get children involved in cooking.

Rev. Ken Fleck

Bran Muffins

2 c. bran buds
2 c. boiling water
1 c. shortening
2-1/2 c. sugar
4 eggs
1 qt. buttermilk
5 t. baking soda
1 t. salt
4 c. All-Bran cereal
5 c. flour

Mix bran buds with 2 c. boiling water. Cream shortening and sugar. Add eggs, buttermilk, baking soda, salt, All-Bran, and flour. Combine creamed mixture and bran buds. Drop into greased muffin pan; fill only halfway.

Bake at 400 degrees for 15 minutes.

Rev. Bernard Kennedy, OFM

Corn Bread

There are many boxed mixes on the market with easy directions and corn bread is a wonderful variation of bread to serve with almost any meal. This is my favorite version from scratch. Corn bread can also be made over a camp fire in a skillet and served with plenty of butter and/or honey.

1 c. yellow corn meal
1 c. flour
2 T. sugar
4 t. baking powder
1/2 t. salt
1 c. milk
1/4 c. vegetable oil
1 egg

Beat milk, oil and egg in a medium sized bowl. Sift dry ingredients together. Add to liquid ingredients and mix well. Pour into a greased 8x8x2 inch pan or pie pan. Bake at 425 degrees for 20 to 25 minutes (Time varies according to pan size.).

Corn Muffins are easily made from this same recipe but use the muffin tins greased or lined with paper cups. Bake 12 to 14 minutes.

Rev. Ken Fleck

Banana Bread

1/4 c. shortening
1/2 c. sugar
1 egg
1 t. vanilla
1/2 t. baking soda
1/2 t. salt
1-1/2 c. ripe bananas, mashed
1 c. All-Bran
1-1/2 c. flour
1/2 c. nut meats (walnuts, pecans, etc.)

Combine shortening, sugar, and egg. Add vanilla, soda, and salt. Stir in bananas and All-Bran. Add flour and nuts. Place in greased and floured bread pan. Bake at 350 degrees for about an hour.

Rev. Bernard Kennedy, OFM

Corn Bread & Variations

1-1/2 c. cornmeal
3/4 c. flour
1 t. salt
1 c. milk
3 T. vegetable oil
1 egg, beaten
2 t. baking powder

Mix all the ingredients together. Bake in a preheated oven at 400 degrees for 15 to 25 minutes.

> —in preheated cast iron molds, 15 to 18 minutes
> —in muffin tins, 20 minutes
> —in cold baking pan, 25 minutes
> —in preheated cast iron pan, 25 minutes

Variations

Corny Corn Bread

Add one can (1-1/2 c.) drained whole kernel corn or fresh or frozen.

Country Corn Bread

Add 1-1/2 c. crisp fried and crumbled bacon bits or 1-1/2 c. crumbled pork rinds or cracklin.

South of the Border Corn Bread

Add 1 c. whole kernel corn as above and 1/2 c. finely chopped red and green peppers. For spice use Jalapeno peppers.

Jumping Jack Corn Bread

Shred or dice 4 oz. Jalapeno hot pepper cheese, and mix into dough.

Rev. Ken Fleck

Your Variations

Corn Sticks

I got a set of corn stick cast iron molds, and there are many other molds that can be used as well and picked up inexpen - sively from flea markets. The hardest part of this recipe is keep - ing them on hand and avoiding getting a burn from the hot iron molds.

Preheat the oven to 450 degrees. Grease the corn stick molds (I use vegetable oil and a brush. A spray vegetable oil can be used as well.) Then prepare the batter.

1-1/2 c. corn meal
1/2 c. flour
3 t. baking powder
1 t. sugar
1 t. salt
1/2 t. baking soda
1/4 c. vegetable oil
1-1/2 c. milk
1 egg

Stir all ingredients together and mix well for at least one minute. After iron molds are hot, 10 minutes in oven, add batter. (Use thick pads as these irons transfer heat quickly.) Fill 2/3 full. Bake at 450 degrees for 12 to 14 minutes. It will start to turn golden brown when done.

Rev. Ken Fleck

Corn Bread Dressing

Crumble up one baked pan of corn bread.

Add:

> 1 medium diced onion
> 2 large ribs of celery diced
> 1/2 c. chopped parsley
> 1 t. salt
> 1 T. poultry seasoning
> 1 t. pepper, fresh ground
> 1 stick margarine,
> > melted & allowed to cool but not solidify
> 2 eggs, beaten
> 1/2 to 1 c. turkey or chicken broth.

> *(Heart healthy suggestion, use low sodium, low fat*
> *canned broth, add more broth and skip the margarine.)*

Mix all ingredients together. Blend well. Place in a casserole dish and place in preheated oven at 375 degrees about 20 minutes until slightly brown, crusty, and hot.

Rev. Ken Fleck

Irish Soda Bread

3 c. flour
2/3 c. sugar
1 T. baking powder
1 t. baking soda
1 t. salt
2 eggs
1-1/2 c. buttermilk
2 T. melted butter
1-1/2 c. moist raisins or currants

Sift dry ingredients, add slightly beaten eggs, buttermilk, and butter. Mix, until all is moist. Add raisins or currants. Bake at 350 degrees for 50 to 60 minutes in a greased loaf pan. If raisins are hard, soak in hot water for 5 minutes and dry them before adding to batter.

Rev. Jerry Williams, O. Carm.

To substitute for buttermilk — mix 1-1/2 T. vinegar in 1-1/2 c.
regular milk and let it stand a while.

Cranberry Nut Bread

2 c. flour, sifted
1 c. sugar
1-1/2 t. baking powder
1/2 t. baking soda
1/2 t. salt
2 to 3 T. shortening
grated rind of 2 to 3 oranges
1 c. orange juice, freshly squeezed if possible
1 or 2 beaten eggs (about 1/3 c.)
1-1/2 c. raw cranberries, halved
3/4 c. nuts, chopped

Sift dry ingredients together. Cut in shortening. Blend in orange rind, juice, and egg. Mix well. Fold in cranberries and nuts. Pour into a greased 9x5x3 inch loaf pan or greased muffin tins. Bake at 350 degrees for 1 hour for a loaf and 20 to 22 minutes for muffins.

Rev. Robert H. Oldershaw

Sweet Soda Bread

I came up with the recipe because I misread my mother's recipe. If you want ordinary soda bread, skip the raisins and caraway seeds and use 2 T. of sugar instead. But then, who wants to be ordinary? This version of soda bread is much sweeter and more like coffee cake.

4 c. flour
2 c. sugar
1 T. baking powder
2 t. baking soda
2 c. raisins
1 T. caraway seeds
2 c. buttermilk

Preheat oven to 300 degrees. Mix all the ingredients. Fold in the buttermilk. Best baked in two 9-inch cast iron skillets. Bake at 300 degrees for 45 minutes to 1 hour.

Rev. John T. Boyle

Banana Muffins

1-1/3 c. sugar
3 eggs
1-1/2 c. corn oil
2 c. ripe bananas, the riper the better
2-1/4 c. flour
2 t. baking soda
1 t. salt
2 t. cinnamon
1 c. nuts, chopped
1 small can (2/3 c.) crushed pineapple
1 c. of raisins, soaked in water then drained
coconut (optional)

Grease muffin pans or use cup cake papers. Makes 36 muffins. Preheat oven to 350 degrees. Bake for 15 to 20 minutes.

Rev. Edmund J. Schreiber by Shirley Tadevic

German Light Rye Bread

6 cans beer (72 oz.)
6 t. celery flakes or seed
5 t. caraway seed
6 t. salt
3 T. dry yeast
1-1/2 T. corn syrup
1-1/2 T. corn oil
8 eggs
4 c. dry milk
3 c. rye flour
18 c. white flour

Boil beer, celery flakes or seed, caraway seed, and salt. Let cool. Add yeast, corn syrup, corn oil, eggs, dry milk, rye flour, and white flour. Mix. Let double. Punch down and divide into loaves. Let rise and bake at 350 degrees for 55 minutes.

Rev. Bernard Kennedy, OFM

Crepes

Another easy as pancakes recipe to make, yet so many avoid them because we associate this easy dessert with finer restaurants and expensive prices. I got this recipe from a family I stayed with in La Ferte-sous-Jouarre, Seine-et-Maine, France, just outside of Paris in 1974.

2 c. flour
2 T. sugar
1/2 t. baking powder
1/2 t. salt
2 c. milk
2 eggs
3 T. melted butter
1 T. cognac or brandy or vanilla

Mix all ingredients into one bowl. Beat until smooth. (This can also be done with a mixer.) Batter should be thin in consistency so that it spreads quickly in a hot pan to cover the surface.

For each crepe, lightly butter an 8-inch pan. A non-stick pan can be used to reduce the butter used. Cook over a medium high heat. Preheat the pan until water drops dance on hot surface. Pour just 1/4 c. of batter, about one large mixing spoon, of batter into the hot pan. Rotate the pan immediately coating the whole pan with the batter. (If it does not move quickly to coat the pan, the batter may be too thick. Thin with a little milk.) Cook until lightly brown. Flip with a fork or spatula to lightly cook the other side. This happens in a matter of 15 to 20 seconds.

Cook and set aside until all the crepes are prepared and stacked on one another. Keep covered while cooling to prevent drying out.

Take each crepe and spread with your favorite marmalade: orange, strawberry, raspberry. Roll up on a plate to be served two to three per person. Lightly dust with powdered sugar.

A Paris Variation:

Spread with a nut chocolate mixture called "Nutella", it can also be garnished with chopped pecans, and dusted with powdered sugar.

Rev. Ken Fleck

The French traditionally fold their crepes twice forming a quarter circle.

Crepes Variations

Like the pancake variations it is limited only by your imagination. Any fresh fruit may be used in due season and wrapped in this delicate blanket. The crepes can be made ahead of time and kept in an airtight container until ready for use at the meal. They can be served hot or cold.

Use your favorite pie filling, heated or cold—cherry, blueberry, apple, pineapple, etc.

Dust with cinnamon sugar or powdered sugar.

Garnish with whipped cream, and red and green seedless grapes dusted with powdered sugar.

If serving on a hot summer day, use the cold pie filling or fresh fruit and freeze the grapes ahead of time, lightly dusting with powdered sugar and putting a small cluster with each dessert.

Rev. Ken Fleck

Crepes Suzette

Sauce:
>   1/2 c. butter
>   2/3 c. orange juice
>   1/4 c. sugar
>   1/3 c. orange liquor

Flambé:
>   1/3 c. brandy

In a 10-inch non-stick pan or a chafing dish combine first four ingredients. Bring to a slow boil then reduce the heat to simmer the sauce.

Fold each crepe separately, brown side facing down, first in half, then in half again. This gives you a quarter circle. Do this for each crepe and place in the sauce that is simmering. Spoon the sauce over the crepes.

Heat the brandy in a separate container. Flame and pour over the crepes in the pan, spooning the liquid over the crepes until it is absorbed.

Serve two crepes per person and dust with powdered sugar.

Rev. Ken Fleck

Crazy Crust Pizza

1 pkg. mild Italian sausage
1 pkg. hot Italian sausage

Fry together, drain and let stand for a while.

Batter (will be wet):
>   **1 c. flour**
>   **2 eggs**
>   **2/3 c. milk**
>   **1 t. salt**
>   **1 t. oregano**

Mix well with a fork. Put on a greased cookie sheet. Tip sheet to coat all the edges. Put meat on batter along with vegetables of choice. Bake for 25 minutes at 425 degrees. Take out and spread pizza sauce on top and cover with shredded cheese. Return to oven for 10 minutes.

Rev. Jerry Williams, O. Carm.

Donna Gibbon's Spinach Bread

1 pkg. of 2 loaves of frozen white bread dough
1 pkg. frozen chopped spinach, cooked and drained
1-1/2 lbs. bulk Italian sausage, cooked and drained
1 lb. shredded Mozzarella cheese
3/4 c. Parmesan cheese
garlic powder to taste
oregano to taste

Thaw bread according to package directions and allow to rise. Combine drained sausage, drained spinach, cheese and spices together. Roll individual loaves of dough into 9x12-inch rectangles. Place half the filling down the center of each rectangle, up to an inch from the edge. Bring sides together and pinch at the top. Fold the ends under. Brush pastry with egg whites and form them into a crescent shape. Place each crescent on a cookie sheet and bake at 325 degrees for 25 minutes. This bread freezes well.

Rev. Jerry Williams, O. Carm.

Franciscan Brown Bread

3 packets dry yeast
6 c. warm water
2/3 c. molasses
2 oz. shortening
2 t. salt
2-1/2 c. whole wheat flour
1-1/2 c. medium rye flour
9 c. white flour

In a bowl, combine yeast, water and molasses. Add shortening and dry ingredients. Mix until doughy. Divide into round loaves and let rise. Bake at 375 degrees for 1 hour.

Rev. Bernard Kennedy, OFM

Elizabeth Bread

This is a great breakfast sweet bread and is a perfect Christmas bread. This bread is named after my goddaughter who loves this recipe. I think this bread can be made in the conventional way, but since I only use the bread machine, you're on your own.

5-1/2 oz. milk, 90-100 degrees (or lukewarm)
2 large eggs, lukewarm
2 t. orange or lemon extract
2 t. butter flavoring (McCormick seasoning)
3 cups bread flour
1-1/2 T. butter
2-1/2 T. sugar
1-1/2 t. salt
2 t. cinnamon (optional)
1/2 cup golden raisins (optional)
1/2 cup dark raisins (optional)
2 t. active dry yeast

Place all liquid ingredients in bread pan. Add all dry ingredients, putting yeast in last after forming a well in middle of dry ingredients. Use basic setting on bread machine and light or medium crust setting. Place raisins in when machine beeps for additional ingredients. Makes 1-1/2 lb. loaf.

Rev. Richard J. Prendergast

Irish Soda Bread

2 eggs, beaten
1-3/4 c. buttermilk
2 T. melted butter
2/3 c. sugar
1 T. baking powder
1 t. baking soda
1 t. salt
3 c. flour
1/2 c. raisins

Cream eggs, buttermilk, and melted butter. Add dry ingredients and mix well. Grease a 5 x 9 loaf pan. Put dough in pan. Bake at 350 degrees for 1 hour.

Rev. Bernard Kennedy, OFM

Muffins Galore

The recipe for muffins is easy and makes a wonderful start to the day with breakfast.

Quick Start Tips:

Keep a canister of the basic muffin dry ingredients on hand.

Use paper muffin cups for your muffin tin to make clean up a snap.

1 egg
1 c. milk
1/4 c. vegetable oil
2 c. flour
1/2 c. sugar
2 t. baking powder
1/2 t. salt

Beat together, egg, milk, and oil. Sift dry ingredients together. Mix dry ingredients into liquids lightly—just until the dry ingredients are moistened (20 to 25 strokes). Batter will be lumpy. Using a muffin tin either grease the tin or use muffin paper cups to line them. Fill cups 2/3 full. Bake at 400 degrees for 20 to 25 minutes. Remove from pan to a cooling rack.

Rev. Ken Fleck

Variations on Mike's Muffin Madness

Blueberry

Fold into batter 1 c. fresh or frozen blueberries. Frozen blueberries only need to be rinsed, not thawed, before adding.

Apple

When mixing liquids add 1 c. grated apple. Add 1 t. cinnamon to the dry ingredients.

Bran

Decrease flour to 1 c. and substitute 1-1/2 c. Bran buds or 2 c. bran flakes or 1 c. bran flour, or wheat flour, or oat flour (easily made by putting oat meal in a blender).

Orange/Cranberry

Add 1 c. cranberries coarsely chopped or chopped in a blender/food processor, and add 1/3 c. frozen orange juice concentrate to liquid ingredients or 2 T. grated orange rind.

Banana Nut

Add two small, ripe mashed bananas *(Black banana peels means the sugar has left the skin and entered the fruit as it ripens—wonderful!)* to liquid ingredients and 1/2 c. chopped pecans or walnuts.

Rev. Ken Fleck

Chocolate Chip Cupcakes

4 c. flour
2 c. sugar
5 t. baking powder
1 t. salt
3 eggs
1-1/2 c. milk
1 c. vegetable oil
2 t. vanilla extract
2 c. or one 12 oz. package of chocolate chips

Sift flour, sugar, baking powder and salt twice. Set aside. Beat eggs, milk, oil, and vanilla in a large bowl. Add dry ingredients, chips, and mix just until moistened.

Coat the muffin tin cups with shortening or a vegetable spray or line tins with paper cups. Spoon batter into muffin tin filling each cup 2/3 full. Bake at 350 degrees for 25 to 30 minutes until lightly brown on top. Let cool a few minutes then remove from muffin tin to a cooling rack before storing.

Makes about 30 muffins.

Rev. Ken Fleck

A Prayer for Dinner Parties

A woman invited some people to dinner. At the table, she turned to her six-year old daughter and said, *"Would you like to say the blessing?"*

"I wouldn't know what to say," she replied.

"Just say what you hear Mommy say," the mother said.

The child bowed her head and said, *"Dear Lord, why on earth did I invite all these people to dinner?"*

Pumpkin Muffins

1-1/2 c. whole wheat flour
1/2 c. all purpose flour
1-1/2 t. baking powder
1/2 t. baking soda
1/2 t. salt
1/2 t. ground cinnamon
1/2 t. ground nutmeg
1/2 t. ground cloves
2 eggs, slightly beaten
1 c. canned pumpkin (16 oz.)
1/2 c. sugar
1/2 c. milk
1/4 c. cooking oil
1 c. raisins
1/2 c. chopped nuts of your choice

Stir together both flours, baking powder, baking soda, salt, cinnamon, nutmeg, and cloves. Set the mixture aside. Preheat oven to 400 degrees. Stir together in second bowl, the eggs, pumpkin, sugar, milk, and oil. Add flour mixture to pumpkin mixture, stirring until dry ingredients are moist. Batter will be lumpy. Gently stir in raisins and nuts. Grease pans or use paper baking cups. Bake for 15 minutes or until golden brown. Makes 18 cups.

Rev. Edmund J. Schreiber

Short Cut Super Breads

Sometimes cooks would like something special to enhance an ordinary meal. Nothing adds sparkle to a meal like warm, creative bread. We don't always have time to bake bread from scratch. Here's where cheating is allowed taking advantage of new food items as well as creative short cuts.

Using your favorite bread loaf e.g., French, Vienna, Rye, hoagie rolls, Kaiser rolls, etc. Slice rolls in half and loaves should be sliced in 1 inch slices on an angle. Spread with one of the following. Reassemble the bread and wrap in aluminum foil. Place in the oven 15-20 minutes before your meal is served while the oven is still hot or heat at 300 degrees.

Bread Spreads

1. See recipe for Great Gobs of Garlic.
2. Into 2 sticks of butter or margarine add one of the following:
   - Snipped chives.
   - Seeds of various sorts, poppy, celery, caraway, sesame.
   - 1 t. garlic or onion salt.
   - 3 T. grated Parmesan cheese and 1/2 t. oregano or Italian seasoning.
3. Soft cheese spreads of all sorts that can he purchased at grocery stores.

Rev. Ken Fleck

Basic Yeast Bread

1-1/3 c. warm water 110-120° F.
>   *(Test with your finger. It should be warm, not hot to your touch.)*

1 t. sugar
1 packet (2-1/2 t.) of yeast
2 T. extra virgin olive oil
1 t. salt
3-3/4 to 4 c. bread flour
>   *(You can use all purpose flour but high gluten flour will give you better results.)*

In a small bowl dissolve sugar in warm water. Add yeast. Let it start to rise. If it doesn't start to rise after five minutes, your yeast may be bad. Start over.

Add the oil and salt to the liquid. Gradually add flour to the liquid, mixing it in. When it becomes difficult you may continue kneading the dough in a large strong bowl or on a breadboard or on a table covered with a pastry cloth or large towel. To hold a breadboard in place, put a towel underneath it.

Put the dough in a clean lightly greased bowl and cover. Let it rise for 1-1/2 to 2 hours in a warm place. Then mold or form into the shapes you want. The dough can also be left in the refrigerator overnight and used the next day. Punch it down if it rises too far. The refrigerator will slow down the rising process but not stop it.

Tips:

— For a tighter loaf of bread use half as much yeast. Let the dough rise slowly 2 - 3 times. It will give the bread a different texture.

— To create a thick, dense, chewy crust, place a pan of water on the floor of the oven. It will inject moisture into the oven as it bakes.

— Cool the bread on a rack. This will help the crust to be consistent all around.

— Brush finished loaves with butter for a soft top.

— Do not slice bread for hour. It is still baking and settling inside. Then use a sharp serrated knife while laying the loaf on its side.

Rev. Ken Fleck

Bagels

1/4 c. warm water
pinch of sugar
1 pkg. dry yeast

Start yeast separately to make sure it works.
2 c. warm water
1/2 c. vegetable shortening
4 T. sugar
1 t. salt
5-6 c. high gluten flour

In a large mixing bowl add water, shortening, sugar, malt sugar, and salt. Add flour, 1 to 2 c. at a time and stir in until batter is smooth and starts to leave the sides of the bowl. Dough will be sticky and elastic. Knead in remaining flour until it is still sticky.

Butter the sides of a bowl for rising. Place dough in the bowl. Brush top of dough with butter. Butter one side of plastic wrap and cover bowl with buttered side down. Cover with a towel and allow to rise in a draft-free place for one hour. Punch down and allow to rise another 1 to 1-1/2 hours or overnight.

Work on a floured surface. Divide dough in half. Half may be kept for up to three days for second set of five bagels.

Divide dough into five equal parts. Keeping the surface well-floured, knead each piece of dough until it forms a small ball that is smooth and well-floured. Flatten each ball and punch a hole in the middle. Enlarge the hole until it is about as large as the ball was. This allows for the next rising of the dough to close the hole. Allow to rise on a floured towel.

Bring water to a boil in a large, wide pot. Place bagels into boiling water. They will sink then rise. Allow to cook in the water for about 1-1/2 minutes each side. Remove to a towel to dry.

Place on a surface that has cornmeal and perhaps some of your seeds for top coating on it. It gives the bottom side flavor as well as the top.

While still warm coat each bagel with the white of an egg that has been strained. This gives you a white product that has the gelatinous portion removed for a smoother glaze. You can decorate bagels with a variety of seeds: sesame, caraway, poppy, etc.

Continued on next page

Bagels (Cont'd.)

Bring an oven to 500 degrees to heat baking tiles placed on rack. Slide the bagels onto the tiles to bake, and put 6 to 8 ice cubes on the floor of the oven to give moisture to the oven. Reduce heat to 450 degrees and bake for 20 minutes. Turn oven off and allow to sit in cooling oven for 5 minutes. Open door slightly and allow to sit another 5 minutes. Allow to cool for 15 minutes before eating.

Spread:

Use soft whipped cream cheese and add diced vegetables to your taste, e.g. diced carrots, radishes, green pepper, red pepper, green onions, etc. You are limited by your imagination, make it colorful and tasty. Salt and pepper to taste.

Rev. Ken Fleck

Garlic Bread The Italians Never Knew

1/2 lb. (2 sticks) butter or margarine
1/3 c. garlic, minced
2 T. pimento, chopped
2 T. green pepper, finely chopped
1 T. parsley, finely snipped
1 T. Worcestershire sauce
2 T. brandy or Cognac
1 long loaf Italian Bread
Parmesan cheese, grated
paprika (optional)

In a medium bowl mix the softened butter (room temperature) garlic (for convenience I keep a jar of minced garlic in the fridge.), pimento, green pepper, parsley, Worcestershire, and brandy. Mix until all ingredients are well-blended into a smooth spread.

Slice your Italian bread lengthwise so that it fits a cookie sheet that will fit under your broiler 4-5 inches away from the heat. Generously spread the mixture over your bread. Place under broiler for two minutes. Pull out and sprinkle generously with grated Parmesan and for color and taste you may add a sprinkle of paprika. Give it two more minutes under the broiler. Watch so it doesn't burn. Slice diagonally.

This and a hearty soup is a meal in itself.

Rev. Ken Fleck

Hazelnut and Orange Biscotti

2 c. unbleached all purpose flour
1/4 t. baking powder
1/4 t. baking soda
1/4 t. salt
3 large eggs
2/3 c. vanilla sugar
1 t. pure vanilla extract
1 t. almond extract
grated zest of 1 lemon
grated zest of 1 orange
1 c. hazel nuts (4 oz)
1 egg mixed with 1/4 t. salt for egg wash

Preheat oven to 350 degrees. Line a baking sheet with baking parchment. Set aside.

Sift together flour, baking powder, baking soda, and salt. In a small bowl combine the eggs, sugar, extracts, and zests. Make a well in the center of the flour and add the liquids slowly, drawing the flour into the liquid and mixing with your hands. If necessary, add additional flour to form a firm workable dough. Add the hazelnuts and work them evenly into the dough.

Divide the dough into two equal parts. Pat into two oval cylinders about 2 inches by 12 inches and transfer to the parchment-lined baking sheet. Evenly brush the dough with the egg wash. Place the baking sheet in the center of the oven and bake at 350 degrees until the dough is slightly risen and an even light golden brown, 25 to 30 minutes. Remove to a cooling rack for 10 minutes.

Transfer each cylinder to a cutting board and slice the biscotti on a sharp angle, 45 degrees at 1/2-inch intervals. Stand the biscotti upright on the baking sheet about 1/2 inch apart. Return the baking sheet to the center of the oven and bake another 15 minutes until the biscotti are a deep golden brown. Remove from the oven and transfer to a cooling rack to be thoroughly cooled.

Cookies should be dry and crispy. They may be stored in a cool dry container for up to a month.

Rev. Ken Fleck

Apple Cinnamon Baked French Toast

1 large loaf French bread
8 extra large eggs
3-1/2 c. milk
1 c. sugar
1 T. vanilla
3 t. cinnamon
1 t. nutmeg
6 to 8 medium-sized cooking apples
     (Cortland, McIntosh, or Granny Smith)
1/8 stick butter

Slice bread into 1-1/2 inch thick slices. Spray 9x13-inch glass pan with corn oil or non-stick spray. Place bread in glass dish, placing tightly together.

In a separate bowl, beat together 1/2 c. sugar, milk and vanilla (by hand, with whisk, for about 30 seconds). Pour one half of egg/milk mixture over bread.

Peel, core, and slice apples. Cover the bread with apple slices. Pour balance of milk/egg mixture evenly over apples.

Mix remaining 1/2 c. sugar with cinnamon and nutmeg and sprinkle mixture evenly over apples. Dot with butter. Cover and refrigerate overnight.

Next Day:

Preheat oven to 350 degrees. Uncover dish and bake in oven 1 hour. It will rise high and brown nicely. Remove from oven and allow to rest for 5 to 10 minutes before serving. Cut into squares and serve with heated syrup, plus smoked sausage, bacon, or your favorite breakfast meat.

Rev. Rich Sztorc

Shepherd's Bread

2 c. unbleached flour
1 c. high gluten flour
1-1/2 t. salt
1-1/4 c. lukewarm water (110-120 degrees)

Preheat your oven to 450 degrees.

Combine all ingredients and with your hands mix all ingredients thoroughly. You may not need all the water. Knead the dough on a floured surface until it does not stick to your fingers but is pliable. Divide the dough into about 12 equals balls (Apostolic?). Roll into flattened disks with your hand. Place on a breadboard or pastry cloth and with a rolling pin and extra flour to keep them from sticking, roll as thin as you can.

Place on an ungreased cookie sheet and bake for 2 to 5 minutes on one side, until lightly browned, then turn over with tongs and cook for another 2 minutes. The bread will be bumpy with air pockets. Don't let it burn. This bakes quickly. Cool on a wire rack and serve immediately with your favorite spreads or appetizers.

The same recipe can be used for Eucharistic bread. Substitute whole wheat flour for half the total. When making the disks roll to about 1/4 inch thickness. Bake at 450 degrees for 8 to 10 minutes. You do not want it to bake out all the moisture. You can make the disks as large as necessary for different Masses. One disk will usually give you about 20 to 25 portions.

Rev. Ken Fleck

Irish Soda Bread

1 c. sugar
2 sticks margarine, melted
6 c. all purpose flour
2 t. baking soda
1 t. baking powder
1/2 t. cream of tartar
1 t. salt
3 c. buttermilk
1 c. (heaping) dark raisins
1 c. (heaping) light raisins

In a large bowl blend together the sugar and margarine. In a another large bowl blend the flour, baking soda, baking powder, cream of tartar, and salt.

Add 2 c. of flour mixture to the sugar/margarine bowl. Blend in 1 c. buttermilk. Blend well. Add 2 more c. flour mixture and 1 c. buttermilk. Blend well. Add remaining 2 c. flour mixture and 1 c. buttermilk. Blend well. Fold in raisins.

Place the batter equally into 3 greased 5x9 inch loaf pans. Bake at 350 degrees for 1 hour.

Rev. William J. Devine

Irish Soda Bread

This recipe I submitted at the Irish Fest held a year after I became pastor of St.George. Not wanting to taint the judges' opinion I submitted my recipe under the pseudonym of Mary O'Shea. To my surprise "Mary O'Shea" won first place. I hope you find a winner in this recipe as well.

3 C. flour
1/2 C. sugar
1 T. baking powder
1 t. baking soda
2 C. dried cherries and golden raisins
2 C. buttermilk
2 large eggs
3 T. melted butter
1 t. vanilla extract

Sift together the flour, sugar, baking powder, baking soda. Add the dried cherries and golden raisins to the sifted ingredients. In a large bowl, beat buttermilk, eggs, 2 tablespoons of the butter and vanilla extract until blended. Add the dry ingredients to these liquid ingredients. Stir until evenly moistened. Do not over stir.

In a 10-inch cake pan that has been greased and prepared with a piece of parchment paper in the bottom, spread the batter. (You may also use a cheesecake pan with a removable bottom.) Drizzle with the remaining butter. Bake at 350 degrees 45 - 50 minutes or until evenly browned and a toothpick inserted in the center comes out clean. Allow to cool in the pan for 15 minutes before removing to a cooling rack. This can also be baked in a loaf pan of choice as well. Serve warm with butter or at room temperature.

Rev. Ken Fleck

Day Four

Looks too plain...I know!
Let's add some sprinkles!

"God said, 'Let there be lights in the vault of heaven to divide the day from night, and let them indicate festivals, days and years. Let there be lights in the vault of heaven to shine on the earth.' And so it was. God made the two great lights: the greater light to govern the day, the smaller light to govern the night, and the stars."

Genesis 1:14-17

Pasta & Rice

Michael's Delight: Ziti with Meat Sauce

1 box ziti
1 lb. Italian sausage
1 lb. ground beef
1-1/2 qt. spaghetti sauce
1 lb. mozzarella cheese
16 oz. Polly-0 ricotta cheese

Boil ziti until tender. Take casing off sausage. Place sausage and ground beef in large pan, break up clumps of meat. Cook for 10 minutes. Pour in tomatoes or spaghetti sauce. Cook until meat is done.

Line up ziti in a pan in a layer, press ziti down and cover with meat and sauce. Spread ricotta over meat and dice some mozzarella and sprinkle over ziti. Put another layer of ziti and repeat as above. Put in as many layers of ziti and meat sauce as you wish. Since everything is cooked, you can just heat it and sprinkle some mozzarella cheese diced over the top.

Don't add cheese while it is cooking to avoid burning cheese.

Rev. Thomas S. Boyle

Pun with Monks

Lost on a rainy night, a nun stumbles across a monastery and requests shelter there. Fortunately, she's just in time for dinner and was treated to the best fish and chips she's ever had.

After dinner, she goes into the kitchen to thank the chefs.

She is met by two brothers, "Hello, I'm Brother Michael, and this is Brother Charles."

"I'm very pleased to meet you. I just wanted to thank you for a wonderful dinner. The fish and chips were the best I've ever tasted. Out of curiosity, who cooked what?"

Brother Charles replied, "Well, I'm the fish friar."

She turns to the other brother and says, "Then you must be…?"

"Yes, I'm the chip monk."

Noodle Rice Casserole

1 stick margarine
8 oz. very fine noodles
2 c. instant rice
2 cans onion soup
2 cans chicken broth
1 c. mushrooms
1 can water chestnuts
1 t. soy sauce
1 c. water or white wine

Brown noodles in margarine. Mix all ingredients and place in 9 x 13 inch pan. Cover with foil and bake in 350 degrees oven for 40 to 50 minutes.

Rev. Richard Ehrens

Nick's Fettuccini

fresh fettuccini pasta
your favorite Alfredo sauce
1/4 lb. smoked salmon filet
1/4 c. black caviar

Make your favorite Alfredo sauce as the pasta cooks. Drain the pasta and coat well with Alfredo sauce. Divide onto warm plates, and on top of each serving, sprinkle finely diced salmon and a sprinkling of caviar. Unbelievable taste sensation!

Rev. Jerry Williams, O. Carm.

Pasta Aglio Olio with Garlic and Oil

Any pasta noodle (linguine, spaghetti, etc.)
1/4 c. fresh garlic, chopped
1/4 c. parsley flakes, chopped
1/2 c. olive oil
grated Romano or Parmesan cheese to taste

Cook pasta approximately 20 minutes after bringing water to a boil. Warm oil, parsley, and garlic together. Don't make the oil too hot or the garlic will burn and become bitter. Drain the pasta and pour oil mixture over it. Optional: add 2 T. of water to lessen the oiliness if preferred. Add salt and pepper and grated cheese. (Romano, Parmesan to taste)

Rev. Mike Solazzo

Penne Arrabiata (biblical style)

1/3 c. extra virgin olive oil
3 t. minced garlic (or to taste)
1/4 lb. of thick sliced bacon or Italian pancetta, diced
1 large can (15 oz.) Italian style plum tomatoes
1/3 c. dry red wine
1/3 t. dried red pepper flakes
1/2 t. cracked black pepper
2 T. minced basil
1 lb. penne rigate (small tubular pasta)
pinch of salt (optional)
1 c. grated Parmesan cheese
           (or better, a mixture of Romano and Parmesan)

Heat olive oil in large skillet until moderately hot. Add garlic until it begins to turn brown. Add diced bacon or pancetta and cook until brown but not crunchy. Add tomatoes but break into large pieces with fork or spatula. Add wine, dry red peppers, dash of cracked black pepper. Simmer covered for about 30 minutes until oil begins to rise to top. After 20 minutes add basil and stir in. While sauce is preparing, heat water for pasta in large saucepan (add pinch of salt if desired); when water is boiling, add pasta. Boil about 10 to 15 minutes, until penne is al dente.

When pasta is ready, drain, rinse quickly in cold water, and return to saucepan over low heat. Immediately add sauce and stir until thoroughly mixed and sauce begins to bubble in pasta. Add cheese and mix well into pasta and sauce. Turn off heat and serve, garnish platter with light dusting of additional cheese. Will serve four, but beware, they may come back for more.

Rev. Donald Senior, CP

Swiss Muesli

1-1/2 c. milk
2 c. oatmeal, uncooked
1/4 c. oat bran
1/4 c. grated coconut
2 apples, cored and grated
Juice of 2 lemons
2 T. raw sugar
1/2 c. seedless green or red grapes cut in half
1/2 c. dates, diced
1/2 c. almonds, sliced
1/2 c. soft raisins
1 banana, sliced
1 c. whipping cream
8 strawberries, sliced

In a large mixing bowl, combine milk with the oatmeal, oat bran and grated coconut. Let the mixture stand, stirring once or twice, for about 15 minutes. Sprinkle the apples with the lemon juice and toss with the sugar till well blended. To the apple mixture add the grapes, dates, almonds, raisins, and banana. Then stir the fruit and nut mixture into the oat mixture. Whip the cream and fold half of it into the combined fruit and oat mixture. Spoon into bowls and top with more whipped cream and sliced strawberries. Great for a fancy brunch or a rich dessert.

Rev. Jerry Williams, O. Carm.

Something Very Rice

This is not so much a recipe as it is variations on a theme. Often good cooks serve rice without being creative. Like bread, as a starch, it can be enhanced in many ways depending on the food it is being served with so that the variations compliment the main dish.

Different kinds of rice.

There are many different types of rice used throughout the world that are easily available in our local grocery stores today. Try the different varieties, even mixing different grains once you are familiar with each of the individual flavors.

In the beginning we cook with water following the package recipe. . There is no rule saying that water has to be used. Any liquid will do. Try one of these:

- —Chicken or beef broth. This can also be purchased in low fat and no fat versions, as well as low sodium.
- —Apple juice for half the water.
- —Coconut milk for half the water.
- —Orange juice for half the water.
- —Pineapple juice for half the water.
- —Tomato juice for half the water.

Chinese restaurants are inspirational for a wide variety of flavors and textures to add to rice, which enhance the meal. Try these or create your own in about 4 c. of cooked rice

For crunch and texture:

Add one or a combination of the following:

- —nuts of various sorts: 1/2 c. toasted almonds, pecans, walnuts, toasted sunflower seeds, toasted pine nuts
- —diced carrots, diced celery, diced green pepper, sliced water chestnuts

Continued on next page

Something Very Rice (Cont'd.)

For flavor variation:
- —1/2 c. diced or crumbled crisp bacon
- —1/2 c. diced ham
- —1/2 c. diced chicken or beef
    (good place for leftovers)
- —1 t. curry powder
- —1/2 t. curry & 1/2 t. turmeric
- —1 T. lemon zest (the rind grated)
- —1 T. orange zest
- —1 small can mushrooms (4 oz.) drained and slivered or whole
    from the can
- —1/2 c. stuffed olives sliced
- —3 T. finely chopped onion with 1 clove garlic lightly sautéed in
    butter or 2 T. soy sauce
- —3 T. parsley, chopped finely
- —3 T. red and 3 T. green pepper, finely chopped and sautéed in
    butter.

Rev. Ken Fleck

Stuffing for Turkey or Chicken

1 large bag of corn bread stuffing
2 c. medium celery, cut up
1 very large onion
1/2 c. dark or light raisins
1/2 c. finely chopped carrots
1 c. (or less) chicken stock
1 or 2 T. poultry seasoning
1/2 stick butter

Saute celery, onions, and carrots just until crunchy, in the chicken stock, with 1/2 stick of butter. Stir in raisins, poultry seasons. Add a bit of salt and pepper to taste. Mix all with stuffing. Pour some stock to just moisten. It must be crunchy. Cook for 10 minutes in a 350 degree oven. Serve with gravy.

Rev. Howard Tuite
by Mrs. Christine Radford

Tabbouleh

4 c. boiling water
1 c. Bulgur wheat
2 cucumbers, peeled and chopped
8 radishes, chopped
1/2 c. fresh mint leaves, chopped fine
1/2 c. olive oil
4 fresh green onions, sliced very thin
1/3 c. fresh lemon juice
1/2 t. salt
1/4 t. pepper
1 head Romaine lettuce leaves

Pour the boiling water over the bulgur wheat in a large bowl. Cover the bowl and let stand 2 hours. Drain off any excess liquid. Add the cucumbers, radishes, mint, olive oil, onions, lemon juice, salt, and pepper to the Bulgur. Toss the mixture until all ingredients are thoroughly blended. Refrigerate until ready to serve.

To serve, line a large salad bowl with lettuce leaves and mound the Tabbouleh in the center. Provide a platter of extra lettuce leaves for people to scoop up the Tabbouleh. Nice salad.

Rev. Jerry Williams, O. Carm.

Rigatoni Carbonara (A Roman Specialty)

1 lb. rigatoni pasta
1 stick butter, melted
4 large eggs, beaten
1 lb. cooked and crumbled bacon
1 c. grated Parmesan cheese
fresh ground black pepper

Cook the rigatoni in plenty of salted water. When cooked to proper doneness, (about 15 minutes) drain the pasta and mix it in a large bowl with the melted butter. Add the eggs and mix thoroughly. The eggs will cook on the pasta. Next, add the bacon and cheese and mix. Add pepper to taste. Serve immediately.

Rev. L. J. Cameli

Fettuccini Alfredo

Crème Fraiche:
>   **1/2 pt. whipping cream**
>   **1/3 c. dairy sour cream or 2-1/2 T. buttermilk**

Shake ingredients in a tightly covered jar to blend well. Loosen jar lid, allow to rest in jar. Leave jar at room temp for 8 to 24 hours, or until cream has thickened. (May be kept in refrigerator up to 1 week)

Crème Fraiche
1/2 lb. fettuccini
3 T. unsalted butter
1/2 t. salt
fresh pepper
fresh nutmeg
3/4 c. grated Parmesan cheese

Make crème fraiche one or more days in advance. Cook fettuccine according to the package. Cook al dente; drain.

Meanwhile, stir together over medium heat crème fraiche and butter until butter melts. Add salt, pepper, and nutmeg. Let simmer 1 to 2 minutes. Add fettuccine, stir gently. Simmer about 2 minutes, until fettuccine is hot. Sprinkle with Parmesan. Toss gently.

Makes 2 entrees or 4 appetizers

Rev. Ken Fleck

Santa Chiara Carbonara

3 eggs
1/2 c. Parmesan Cheese
1/4 t. FGP (fresh ground pepper)
1 lb. favorite pasta
1 lb. bacon cooked & crumbled
extra virgin olive oil

Beat the eggs with 1/4 c. Parmesan cheese and FGP. Prepare the pasta according to package (usually 5 qts. boiling water, boil for 7 or 8 minutes, al dente, i.e. firm to the bite). Drain and mix quickly with the beaten egg and cheese mixture and the crumbled bacon. Reheat for about 1 minute, place on a serving platter and garnish with the remaining cheese and FGP to taste. Serves 3-4.

Rev. Ken Fleck

Lemon Rice

5 c. chicken broth
sprig of fresh rosemary
sprig of fresh mint
sprig of fresh sage
grated zest of 1 lemon
4 T. unsalted butter
1 T. extra virgin olive oil
1 medium onion or 2 shallots,
      minced or finely chopped
1-1/2 c. Basmati rice
3 T. lemon juice
1/2 c. grated Parmesan cheese

Bring broth to a simmer in a sauce pan. Chop fresh herbs finely and mix with lemon zest, set aside. In a large, deep skillet, preferably cast iron, combine 2 T. butter, oil and onion over a medium heat. Sauté onion until transparent, about 4 minutes. Add the rice and cook for 2 minutes stirring constantly coating all the grains. Add 1 c. of broth to the rice. Continue stirring until the rice absorbs most of the broth. Continue adding broth gradually and stirring the lightly simmering rice until it is almost all absorbed. This will take about 20 minutes. The rice will have a creamy texture but still be firm—al dente.

Remove from heat and stir in remaining butter, herbs, lemon zest, lemon juice, and Parmesan. Cover and let rest for 5 minutes. Serves 4 to 6.

Rev. Ken Fleck

Orange, Sage, and Mushroom Rice

1 c. (1-1/2 oz) dried mushrooms (porcini or wild sliced)
5 c. boiling water
grated zest of 1 orange
1/2 t. sage
1/4 c. fresh parsley, snipped
1 T. extra virgin olive oil
2 shallots or 1 medium onion, finely chopped
1-1/2 c. Basmati rice
3 T. orange juice
1/2 c. grated Parmesan

Reconstitute the mushrooms in the boiling water for at least 30 minutes or overnight. Squeeze the liquid from them. Rinse and make sure mushrooms are clean. Chop coarsely. Strain liquid and bring to a low simmer in a sauce pan. Combine the orange zest, sage and parsley. Set aside.

In a large, deep skillet, preferably cast iron, combine the oil, 2 T. butter and the onion over medium heat. Sauté the onion until transparent, about 4 minutes. Add the rice, stir until evenly coated, about 2 minutes. Add a cup of the mushroom liquid and continue to cook and stir while it simmers gently and the rice absorbs the liquid. Gradually add the remaining mushroom stock until the rice absorbs most of it, about 20 minutes, stirring regularly. The rice will have a creamy texture but still be firm—al dente. Remove from heat add the remaining butter, orange zest, sage, parsley, orange juice, and cheese. Stir and let rest for five minutes before serving. Serves 4-6.

Rev. Ken Fleck

Notes

Veggies

Ann's Fried Green Tomatoes

I always looked forward to the end of the growing season when tomatoes were in abundance and we would grab the best tomatoes that were still green before the first freeze of fall would ruin them .

Traditional
3 large green tomatoes, just before they ripen
1 egg, beaten
1 c. dry bread crumbs
Enough vegetable oil to cover the bottom of a large skillet with about 1/4 inch of oil.

Heat the oil in the skillet over medium high heat. Clean and dry the tomatoes. Cut the stems out. Slice about 1/2 inch thick (as thick as your little finger). Dip slices into the beaten egg and into the breadcrumbs to coat both sides. Cook in the oil until slightly browned. Salt and pepper to taste. Drain on paper towels.

Lighter Fare
3 large green tomatoes, same as above
1/2 c. flour
1 t. seasoned salt
1 t. basil leaves or oregano
A few good grinds of the pepper mill

Using a nonstick skillet add 3 T. extra virgin olive oil. Cut and prepare the tomatoes as above. Coat with the seasoned flour mixture and cook in the skillet turning only once until lightly browned over medium heat.

Rev. Ken Fleck

Broccoli and Cheese Casserole

20 oz. pkg. frozen broccoli bits
8 oz. cheese whiz
1 stick butter or margarine
Ritz crackers

Boil broccoli until just barely tender, about 5 minutes. Melt cheese and butter together. Put broccoli in a casserole dish, pour on cheese and butter mixture. Crumble Ritz crackers on top of broccoli. Bake at 325 degrees for 25 minutes. Enjoy!

Rev. Joseph W. Seitz

"No Brainer" Bean Casserole

2 (48 oz.) cans pork and beans
1 (16-20 oz.) can kidney beans
1 lb. bacon, fried and chopped
3 tomatoes, chopped
2 green peppers, chopped
1 large onion, chopped
1/2 clove garlic, chopped
Use to taste:
   Louisiana hot sauce
   brown sugar
   chili powder
   ketchup

Mix beans and bacon together cook over low heat or in a slow cooker for 1 hour. Then add the other ingredients. Cook for another hour. Taste. Cook for 1 hour and taste. Cook for 1 more hour and serve.

Rev. John Celichowski, OFM Cap.

Broiled Tomatoes

As the summer season approaches, I always look forward to the fresh full flavor of locally grown tomatoes. The larger varieties are especially good for broiling or grilling.

3 large Beefsteak tomatoes
1/2 c. Parmesan cheese

Wash and dry tomatoes. Cut the stem out. Cut tomatoes in half. Set tomatoes on a cookie sheet or a shallow pan about 6 inches away from broiler or in a covered barbecue grill. After about 5 minutes the tomatoes should be heated through. Remove to sprinkle generously with Parmesan. Place under the broiler or on the grill for another minute or two. Watch so the cheese doesn't burn. When it melts and starts to turn brown, remove to serving tray.

Rev. Ken Fleck

Corn Soufflé

1-1/2 (15 oz.) cans corn (not creamed)
1 stick butter
1/2 c. sugar
1 T. flour
1/2 c. evaporated milk
2 eggs, beaten
1-1/2 t. baking powder
Topping:
    cinnamon
    sugar

Pour corn into blender and blend or grate. At stove, melt butter and sugar in pan. Add flour slowly. Blend in milk, add eggs, then baking powder. Pour all into blender, but do not grate. Mix ingredients with a long spoon. Pour all into a buttered baking dish. Bake in oven at 350 degrees for 30 to 50 minutes, until firmed up. Remove and sprinkle on a mixture of cin-namon and sugar. Optional: red cherries.

Rev. Stanley R. Rudcki

Easy Baked Beans

1/2 lb. thick-cut bacon, cut into pieces
1/2 lb. hamburger
1 onion, chopped
2 or 3 cloves garlic, chopped
4 cans beans, drained and rinsed
      (butter, navy, Northern , kidney, red, black-eyed peas, etc.)
1 c. water
2 – 3 dashes of Worchestershire sauce
4 – 6 T. brown sugar
Tabasco sauce to taste
pepper
salt

In a pot cook the bason, hamburer, onions, and garlic on a medium heat. Add the remaining ingredients, cover and bring to a boil. Reduce heat to simmer and cook for 1-1/2 hours, stirring occasionally. Serve and enjoy.

Rev. Tim Fairman

Greens

Down south and on the southeast side of Chicago everyone knows what *"Greens"* is. It is a wonderful combination of green leafy vegetables. The brighter the color the fresher the greens.

They fall into two categories:

Mild flavored: beet tops, collards, escarole, lettuce (outer leaves), and spinach.

Strong flavored: kale, mustard greens, Swiss chard, and turnip greens.

The mild ones cook quickly in 5 to 10 minutes; the stronger ones take twice as long.

Cleaning the greens requires patience and a lot of water. Remove discolored or brown leaves, and the stems. Wash the greens several times in cold baths of water in your sink or a large bowl so that the sand and grit will fall to the bottom.

In a large 5-6 qt. pot boil 2 lbs. smoked turkey legs or 3 lbs. smoked turkey wings in water that covers the meat for 1 hour or until meat is tender. Remove meat. To the broth, add:

3 lbs. of greens, i.e. 1 lb. mustard, 1 lb. collard, and 1 lb. spinach.

Chop greens coarsely and cook in the turkey broth. The greens will cook down in this order:

— Mustard greens, 20 minutes.

— Then add the collard greens, 10 minutes.

— Then add the spinach, 5 minutes.

— Then add the turkey meat that had been removed from the bones and chopped.

— Add a little vinegar, salt and pepper to taste.

You can use any combination you like. BE CREATIVE!!!

Rev. Ken Fleck

Mashed Potatoes

The potato is probably the starch of choice for the American diet. But we are not limited to the fried potato. Baked potatoes can be garnished in many ways with herded butters and spreads listed in the rice section. Other toppers include sour cream, snipped parsley or chives, your favorite creamed salad dressing, dill, cream cheese, cheddar cheese, jalapeno cheese, etc. BE CREATIVE!!!

For meals many prefer the potatoes mashed, but many balk at the effort required. It is relatively easy with one secret to perfect mashed potatoes— MASH THEM DRY. This gets the lumps out.

2 lbs. potatoes (about 6 medium-sized)
1/2 c. milk
1/4 c. sour cream or butter
salt and pepper to taste

Peel and remove the eyes of the potatoes. Cut into quarters. Cover with salted water and cook until tender about 20 to 25 minutes. Drain and return to medium heat to pull out additional water. Mash the potatoes until no lumps remain. Put some muscle into it. This will take a few minutes. Add the sour cream or butter, and enough milk to bring it to the desired consistency. This will vary.

For a low calorie version omit butter, sour cream and milk. Use fat free chicken broth instead.

Rev. Ken Fleck

Minted Peas

This is a wonderful recipe for holidays and goes well with turkey or lamb.

1 lb. frozen peas
4 T. butter or margarine (1/2 stick)
5-6 oz. mint jelly

Cook peas according to directions. In a small sauce pan over a medium heat melt butter, add jelly. Stir until blended. Pour over peas in a serving bowl and mix to coat peas. Serve immediately.

Rev. Ken Fleck

Orange Glazed Carrots

1 lb. frozen baby carrots
   (Fresh carrots can be used but take longer to cook)
4 T. butter or margarine
5 T. frozen orange juice concentrate
   (Substitute can be 3 T. orange zest*)

Cook carrots according to package directions. If using fresh carrots, clean, cut on an angle to create an attractive shape, about 1/2 inch thick. Cook until tender crisp. Melt butter in a saucepan over a medium heat, add orange juice concentrate or zest. Stir until blended. Pour over the carrots in the serving bowl to mix and coat. Serve immediately. The glaze can be prepared in a microwave also.

*Zest, (not the soap) is the peel of a citrus fruit that is grated.

Rev. Ken Fleck

Red Beans

1 lb. dried red beans
1 large onion diced
3 cloves garlic finely chopped or minced
3 T. parsley, snipped
1 c. celery, diced
2 T. Cajun spices
1 t. cayenne pepper or to taste
1 t. liquid smoke
1 lb. smoked or hot sausage, diced or sliced

Rinse beans and examine for stones and bad ones. In a large pot cover beans with 6 c. water. Bring to a boil for 1 hour adding water, if needed, to keep beans covered with boiling water. Add onions, garlic, parsley, celery, Cajun spices, pepper, and liquid smoke. Let beans continue cooking until soft. Then add sausage and ham. Cook on low heat until creamy. Serve over rice.

Rev. Ken Fleck

Southern Sweet Potato and Apple Casserole

4 or 5 medium sweet potatoes, boiled until tender
2 large apples, peeled and sliced
1/4 stick butter
1/3 c. molasses
1/2 t. salt
2 T. lemon juice
1/4 c. brown sugar
2 T. sugar

Slice potatoes and place half in a greased baking dish. Put sliced apples over potatoes. Mix butter, molasses, salt, lemon juice, brown sugar, and sugar together, then add to the pan. Add the rest of the potatoes. Sprinkle with nuts if you like. Bake 325 degrees for 30 minutes.

Rev. Howard Tuite
by Christine Radford

Spinach Sabina

2 lbs. fresh spinach, washed and stemmed
6 garlic cloves or 2 T. chopped garlic
2 T. extra virgin olive oil
salt and FGP to taste
2 T. fresh lemon juice

In a large pot bring 6 quarts of water to a rolling boil. Add the spinach stirring to cook evenly for just 3 minutes. Drain and rinse in cold water. (*This stops the cooking and helps retain the green color. Most vegetables will retain their color and flavor if plunged into boiling water and cooked for a short period of time.*) Cut the spinach coarsely. Place in a colander and place another bowl on top to press out extra water.

In a large skillet combine the garlic and oil over a medium flame until the garlic starts to turn golden brown, but does not brown, about 3 minutes. Remove and discard the garlic. Add the spinach and toss as it cooks for 2-3 minutes. Salt and pepper to taste. Sprinkle lightly with the lemon juice. Serves 4-6.

Rev. Ken Fleck

Rot Kohl (Red Cabbage)

This is a favorite dish in German restaurants to accompany their heartier meat dishes.

Cabbage is very easy to prepare. Choose a head that is firm and solid. Discard outer discolored leaves. Core and quarter. Cover and cook in 2 c. boiling water with 1 t. salt for about 10 minutes. Shredded cabbage cooks in about half the time. Red cabbage takes almost twice as long to cook and needs 2 T. vinegar in the cooking water. Remove from water and drain.

1 head of red cabbage
5 slices of bacon
1 medium onion sliced thinly
1/3 c. brown sugar
2 T. flour
1/2 c. water
1/3 c. vinegar
1 t. salt
fresh ground pepper to taste

Cook the cabbage as described above. Fry the bacon crisp. Drain and discard most of the fat. Reserve a little to sauté the onion for a few minutes until tender. Stir in the brown sugar and flour. Add the water, vinegar, salt, and pepper. Stirring over medium heat for about 5 more minutes. Add crumbled bacon and onion mixture to the cabbage.

Rev. Ken Fleck

Schaefer Potatoes

6 potatoes, peeled and grated
1 stick butter or margarine
1 beef bouillon cube
salt, pepper, oregano, celery salt, garlic salt

Melt butter or margarine and add potatoes, bouillon cube and spices. Sauté till soft.

Rev. Jerry Williams, O. Carm.

Spinach Quiche

1 tube (5-6 oz.) refrigerator biscuit dough
2 c. (8 oz.) shredded cheese, your choice
2 T. flour
1 c. milk
3 eggs
1/2 t. salt
dash fresh ground pepper
dash nutmeg
1 pkg. (10 oz.) frozen chopped spinach, cooked and drained

In a 9-inch pie pan place biscuits pressing together to form a crust. In a bowl combine the cheese and flour. Add the milk, eggs, salt, pepper, nutmeg, and spinach. Mix well. Pour mixture into the dough lined pie pan. Bake in 350 degree preheated oven for 60 minutes. Serves 6 to 8.

Rev. Ken Fleck

Vera Cruz Tomatoes

3 slices bacon
1/4 c. chopped onion
1/2 lb. fresh spinach, snipped
1/2 c. dairy sour cream
dash hot pepper sauce
4 medium tomatoes
1/2 c. (2 oz.) mozzarella cheese, shredded

Cook bacon till crisp. Drain, reserving 2 T. of drippings. Crumble bacon and set aside. Cook onion in drippings and stir in fresh spinach. Cover and cook till tender, 3 to 5 minutes. Remove from heat. Stir in sour cream, pepper sauce, and bacon.

Cut tops off tomatoes. Remove centers, leaving shells; drain. Sprinkle shells with salt; fill with spinach mixture. Bake in 8"x8"x2" pan at 375 degrees for 20 to 25 minutes. Top with cheese. Heat will melt cheese. Makes 4 servings.

Most Rev. Wilton D. Gregory, Bishop
by Mildred, housekeeper

Zucchini Casserole

3 c. thinly sliced zucchini, unpeeled
1 c. Bisquick
1/2 c. Parmesan cheese
1/2 c. finely chopped onion
1/2 t. parsley
1/2 t. seasoned salt
1/2 t. salt
1/2 t. oregano
dash of pepper
1/2 t. garlic powder
1/2 c. vegetable oil
4 eggs, slightly beaten

Mix all together, spread in a 9 x 13 inch greased pan. Bake at 350 degrees until brown, 25 to 40 minutes. Good appetizer or side dish.

Rev. Jerry Williams, O. Carm.

Zucchini Medley

2 medium (6-8") green zucchini
2 medium yellow zucchini
1 large yellow onion
1 large tomato
3 T. virgin olive oil
1/2 t. Mrs. Dash
1/2 t. sesame seeds (optional)
1/2 t. oregano or Italian seasoning

Cut the zucchini on an angle into 1/4 to1/2 inch slices. Peel onion and dice into large pieces. Chop tomato into 1/2 inch cubes. Heat large, non-stick frying pan with olive oil over medium heat. Add onion and sauté for 2 minutes. Add zucchini. Sauté and toss for 4 minutes. Add tomatoes. Sauté for 2 minutes until heated through. Sprinkle with Mrs. Dash, oregano, and sesame seeds and toss lightly to coat vegetables. Place in serving dish. Serves 6.

Rev. Ken Fleck

Augustinian Asparagus

Young spears, first ones of spring are my favorite and Augustus Caesar's as well.

1 lb. thin green asparagus, trimmed
2 T. butter
1 T. extra virgin olive oil
1/2 c. grated Parmesan cheese

Bring 2 quarts of water to a boil in a large pot. Add the trimmed asparagus and cook until tender-crisp, about 8-10 minutes. Remove the asparagus and plunge into ice cold water to cool down and lock in the flavor. Just for a minute. Remove from cold water and allow to dry. This may be done up to two hours before hand.

When ready to serve heat a large skillet over a medium heat. After it is hot add the olive oil and butter. Add the asparagus and sauté just to bring to serving temperature, 3-4 minutes. Transfer to your serving dish and sprinkle with grated Parmesan cheese.

Rev. Ken Fleck

Broiled Zucchini

5 small young zucchini, about 6-8 inches long
1/4 c. extra virgin olive oil
salt
1 T. fresh thyme

Slice the zucchini lengthwise about 1/4 inch thick. Lightly coat with olive oil and season lightly with salt to taste. Arrange on a cookie sheet. Place 5 inches below broiler in a preheated oven for 2 to 3 minutes until golden brown, turn with a fork or spatula and broil for another 2 to 3 minutes. Arrange on a serving platter, drizzle lightly with the olive oil, sprinkle with fresh thyme. Serve with crusty Italian bread. This can also be done on the grill. Slice the zucchini a little thicker. Watch carefully so it does not burn.

Rev. Ken Fleck

Deep Fried Zucchini and Zucchini Blossom

BATTER:

1/4 c. water
1/4 c. beer, room temperature
1/2 c. flour
2 quarts of peanut oil or cooking oil
3 large egg whites
1 lb. zucchini, sliced 1/4 inch
16 fresh zucchini blossoms picked that morning
   and still closed
2 oz. can anchovies, 16 strips needed
16 strips (3 inch x 1/2 inch) mozzarella cheese

Mix first water, beer, and flour until like a thick pancake batter. Set aside and let rest for 30 minutes.

Preheat oven on lowest setting to keep the batches of fried zucchini warm. Pour the oil into a deep fryer so that the oil is at least two inches deep. Bring oil to 375 degrees.

In a large bowl beat the egg whites until fluffy peaks form. Fold egg whites into batter.

Dip the zucchini by hand into the batter. Allow excess batter to drip off so the slices are evenly coated. Stuff the blossoms with one piece of cheese and one slice of anchovy, close the blossom and dip into the batter.

Carefully lower the blossoms or zucchini into the hot oil a few at a time. This allows them to cook quickly and not absorb the oil. Fry until the zucchini and blossoms are golden brown on all sides. Each batch should only take about 2 minutes. Remove from the oil with a wire skimmer and place on paper towels. Season lightly with salt. Place in pan in oven to keep warm while finishing the other batches. Oil must be consistently hot, 375 degrees, or cooking time will vary. Too hot will burn the coating.

Serve as a hot appetizer or to accompany a main meal.

Rev. Ken Fleck

Eggplant Elise

3/4 c. extra virgin olive oil, divided
1 medium onion, finely chopped
1 T. minced garlic
1 (28 oz.) can of tomatoes, pureed
salt & FGP to taste
1 medium eggplant, 1-inch cubes
1 lb. favorite pasta, uncooked
1/2 lb. mozzarella cheese, cubed

In a skillet combine 1/4 c. oil, the onion and garlic over a medium heat until the garlic starts turning golden brown, about 3 minutes. Add the pureed tomatoes and continue cooking and stirring for 15-20 minutes. Sauce should begin to thicken. Salt and pepper to taste. In another nonstick skillet add the 1/2 c. remaining oil, over a medium high heat. Add cubed eggplant and cook for about 5 minutes. Add salt to taste. Do not add more oil. Eggplant will absorb the oil. Add cooked eggplant to the tomato sauce and reduce to a low heat.

In a large pot bring 3-4 quarts of water to a boil. Add the pasta. Cook until tender but firm — al dente. Drain in a colander thoroughly. Add drained pasta to skillet with eggplant and sauce. Cover and let rest with heat turned off for about 5 minutes. Place in serving bowls and sprinkle with mozzarella, cubed or shredded. Yes, you may substitute parmesan. Don't be afraid to experiment with what tastes best to you.

Rev. Ken Fleck

Spinach (or Broccoli or Asparagus)

olive oil (or any vegetable oil)
2 cloves of minced garlic or 1/4 onion minced
1/2 bag of spinach, washed and rinsed
touch of water

In a sauce pan cover the bottom with olive oil at least so that it swishes. Simmer the minced garlic or onion until barely golden. Put in the spinach and splash in the touch of water. Cover immediately and maintain the heat until you can see steam. Remove from heat and let it cool by itself for 7 to 10 minutes (about 20 minutes for broccoli or asparagus). The broccoli and asparagus would have to be kept on reduced heat.

Rev. Anthony J. Brankin

Celery Polynesian

10 medium celery stalks
1 can (8 oz.) water chestnuts, drained and sliced
1 T. instant chicken bouillon
1/2 t. salt
1/2 t. celery salt
1 t. vegetable oil
1 jar (2 oz.) sliced pimientos, drained

Trim off leaves and root ends from the celery stalks. Remove any coarse strings. Wash the celery. Cut into 1/4 inch diagonal slices. Cook and stir celery, water chestnuts, instant bouillon (dry), salt, and celery salt in oil over medium heat, turning constantly with pancake turner, until celery is crisp-tender, about 10 minutes. Stir in pimiento, heat through. Serves 5.

Br. Robert Fandel, OSM

Sweet-Sour Beans

1-1/2 lbs. green beans, French cut
1 onion, chopped fine
3 T. fresh parsley, minced
3 T. shortening
2 t. paprika
1/4 t. salt
3 T. flour
1/3 c. sugar
1/3 c. vinegar
1 c. milk
1 c. liquid that green beans were cooked in

Cook green beans in salt water. Drain the beans reserving 1 c. of the liquid.

Sauté onion, parsley, & shortening until onions are transparent. Add paprika ad salt. Cook over low heat about 1 minute. Stir in flour and cook 2 more minutes. Add sugar and stir in until dissolved. Add vinegar. Cook until thick and bubbly. Very slowly stir in green bean liquid and milk. (If you do not have enough green bean liquid, add enough milk to make a total of 2 c. of liquid. The sauce will appear to curdle when you add the milk.) Cook over medium heat, stirring constantly, until the sauce is smooth. Add green beans and slowly simmer a few minutes. Serves 6.

Rev. James Kinn

Notes

Day Five

"God said, 'Let the waters teem with living creatures, and let birds fly above the earth within the vault of heaven.' And so it was. God created great sea serpents and every kind of living creature with which the waters teem and every kind of flying creature above the earth."

Genesis 1:20-21

Main Dishes

Baked Ham

The butt portion has a smaller bone and will give you nicer slices. The shank has a larger bone.

Preheat the oven to 325 degrees.

Remove the skin. Score the fat in a diamond pattern and place a whole clove in the center of each diamond. Pour over the ham:

> **1 c. white wine**
> **1 c. 7-Up**
> **1 c. pineapple juice**

Bake 20 to 25 minutes per pound, if thawed, or 40 minutes per pound, if frozen. Baste every 20 to 30 minutes. Cover with aluminum foil when it starts to brown.

30 minutes before baking is finished remove from oven and garnish. Using toothpicks, attach whole pineapple rings with a maraschino cherry placed in the center of each ring. Return to oven to finish baking.

When ham is baked according to the time and weight, remove from oven and let it sit covered with aluminum foil for 15 to 20 minutes. This allows the meat to retain its juices when cut. If cut immediately from the oven, the juices will run out of the meat.

Rev. Ken Fleck

Pizza Pizzazz

ZUCCHINI

Clean a medium green and a medium yellow zucchini. Slice lengthwise about 1/4 inch thick. Sauté in 1 T. extra virgin olive oil in skillet for 1 minute on each side. Arrange on pizza basic crust in an alternating pattern, like petals of a flower. Sprinkle lightly with oregano. Top with thinly sliced or shredded Mozzarella. Bake in oven 5 to 7 minutes

ROASTED GARLIC

Take roasted garlic ("Great Gobs of Garlic" in the Something Different Section), spread thinly on pizza dough. Top with thinly sliced tomatoes, mushrooms, top with mozzarella and sprinkle with grated Parmesan. Bake in oven 5 to 7 minutes.

Rev. Ken Fleck

Barbecued Hamburgers

4 lbs. ground chuck or round (16–20 patties)
1/2 c. bread crumbs
1 egg
2/3 c. chopped onions
1/2 c. chopped celery
2 T. ketchup
2 t. mustard
2 t. pepper
1 t. garlic salt
salt or seasoned salt to taste

Blend all ingredients with meat and form into patties. Flatten the patties as much as possible because the egg and bread crumbs will cause them to expand when cooked. Barbecue over white hot coals to desired doneness. Apply sauce (see below) after turning.

Rev. Robert Kyfes

Barbecue Sauce

1 can condensed tomato soup, undiluted
3 T. vinegar
2 t. mustard
2 T. Worcestershire sauce
1 t. salt
1 t. onion salt
1/2 t. garlic salt
1/2 t. cinnamon
1/2 t. black pepper
1 t. paprika
1 t. chili powder
2 t. sugar

Blend all ingredients into the tomato soup (over a low heat, if desired). Brush on hamburgers while cooling and again when serving.

Rev. Robert Kyfes

Beef Stroganoff

2 T. vegetable oil
2 large onions, chopped coarsely
1/2 lb. sliced mushrooms
2-3 lbs. sirloin steak, partially frozen
1 can Campbell's condensed Golden Mushroom soup
1 jigger (2-3 oz.) brandy or Cognac
5-8 oz. Burgundy wine
3 T. dill pickle relish (any relish will do)
1 tomato, diced

In a nonstick skillet add oil and sauté onions and mushrooms until tender. Remove from skillet to a bowl. Cut the meat, while partially frozen, into 1/2-inch strips, 2-4 inches long. (*It is easier to cut and trim the fat from frozen meat.*) Brown meat in the same skillet over high heat to seal in the juices. After a few minutes the meat should be seared and cooked medium rare. Add the brandy. Be careful as it will flame and burn off the alcohol but leave the flavor. After the blue flames have died down add the wine, soup, the onions and mushrooms, pickle relish, and tomato. Cook a few minutes longer to blend all the flavors and heat the gravy. Serve over noodles.

Rev. Ken Fleck

Baked Chicken Breast

4 chicken breasts, boned and split
bacon slices
lunch beef slices (sold in plastic bags)
1/2 pint sour cream
1 can condensed cream of mushroom soup

Line baking pan with thin slices of dried beef. Roll and wrap chicken breasts with slices of bacon. Place on top of beef slices. Mix together sour cream and soup and pour over chicken. Bake uncovered for 3 hours at 275 degrees.

Rev. Jerry Williams, O. Carm.

Bouillabaisse Ateller

1 (10-1/2 oz.) can condensed cream of celery soup
1 (10-1/2 oz.) can condensed cream of mushroom soup
2 c. half & half
1 pkg. (7 oz.) frozen crabmeat, thawed and well drained
1 pkg. (8 oz.) frozen shrimp, thawed and well drained
1 can baby clams, well drained
1 t. onion salt
1/2 t. black pepper
1 t. Worcestershire sauce
1/4 c. dehydrated onion flakes, chopped
parsley sprigs

With a wire whisk, mix soups and cream together over a very low flame. Stir until all lumps are gone. Stir in remaining ingredients making sure all seafood is well drained. Heat gently to serving temperature and serve hot with a dab of butter and a sprig of parsley. Serves 6-8 people.

Rev. Jerry Williams, O. Carm.

Braised Turkey Wings

3 T. butter
1 large onion, sliced
2 carrots, julienne or bias cut
2 celery ribs, julienne or bias cut
12 cloves fresh garlic, peeled
1 c. dry white wine
2 T. tomato paste
1 t. rosemary
salt
fresh ground pepper
4 turkey wings (legs work as well)

Heat butter in braising pan or flameproof casserole. Add onion, carrots, celery, and let wilt a bit in the pan. Toss garlic, wine, tomato paste, rosemary, salt, and pepper to taste. Arrange turkey wings (tips removed and cut in half) or legs on top and sprinkle with a little more salt and pepper. Cover and cook in a pre-heated 350 degree oven for 1 to 1-1/2 hours, or until tender. Remove cover during last 20 minutes so turkey will brown. Serves 4.

Rev. Ron Gollatz

Firemen's Stuffed Chicken

2 T. butter
2 cloves garlic, pressed
salt and pepper to taste
1 pkg. frozen spinach
6 chicken breasts, pounded between wax paper
small piece feta cheese (2x2 inch)
2 beaten eggs
3/4 c. bread crumbs
1 c. sliced mushrooms
1 T. flour
1 c. white wine
1 c. chicken broth (from 1 cube chicken bouillon)
1 T. lemon juice

Defrost spinach. Squeeze well to drain excess water. Sauté in butter with garlic, salt, and pepper. Be sure liquid has evaporated. Set aside.

Lay chicken breast down. Place spoonful of spinach mixture on top. Cover with small piece of feta cheese. Roll. Toothpick together. Dredge (roll) bundles in beaten eggs. Immediately roll in bread crumbs. Brown in peanut oil. Place in serving pan.

In the frying pan used to sauté spinach, sauté mushrooms. Add flour for roux. Add wine and broth after browning. Cook this liquid down. Add lemon juice. Simmer. Pour over breasts. Serve. There is a bit o' trouble that produces a big taste. Good for company.

Rev. Jerry Rodell

Tomato Pork Chops

8 medium pork chops
2 large onions, sliced
2 green peppers, sliced
2 cans (10-1/2 oz. each) condensed tomato soup
salt and pepper

Brown chops fast in a frying pan. After browning, place in a 9x13 inch baking pan. Add onion to the pan the meat was browned in. Cook until transparent (5 minutes). Add tomato soup. Cook 1 minute. Layer green peppers, salt, and pepper over chops. Now pour soup and onions on top of chops. Cover dish and bake for 45 minutes at 375 degrees.

Rev. Edward R. Fialkowski

Cajun Jambalaya

1/2 lb. lean ham, cubed
1/2 lb. smoked sausage
1 onion, diced
1 clove garlic, chopped
1 can (12 oz.) tomato sauce
2 T. Jambalaya spices
1 T. cayenne pepper
1 c. rice
1/2 lb. shrimp, cleaned and deveined
3 T. vegetable oil

Fry ham and sausage in vegetable oil for a few minutes. Add onion and garlic. When onions are slightly brown add tomato sauce and spices. Simmer over low heat for 13 minutes. Add rice and 2 cups of liquid (including tomato sauce) for every cup of rice. Let simmer over low heat for about 30 minutes. Stir occasionally to keep from sticking to bottom of pan. Add shrimp. When all liquid is absorbed cover and allow to cook for another 10 minutes or until rice is tender.

Serves 8-12

Rev. Ken Fleck

Chicken Cacciatore

4 boneless chicken breasts, thinly sliced
1/4 c. margarine
1 small jar Ragu plain spaghetti sauce
1 large green pepper, thinly sliced
1 medium onion, thinly sliced
cooked rice or pasta

In large fry pan, melt margarine. Over medium high heat, add chicken and cook until no longer pink. Reduce heat to low, add Ragu and simmer covered for 30 minutes. Add green pepper and onion and cook gently until veggies are tender. (about 15 minutes) Serve with hot cooked rice.

Rev. Ken Fleck

Chicken Barcelona

2 (2-1/2 to 3 lb.) chickens, quartered or cut up
1 c. prunes, pitted and quartered
1/2 c. pitted green olives, halved
1/2 c. capers
1/2 c. red wine vinegar
1/2 c. olive oil
2 T. dried oregano
2 T. garlic, crushed or pureed
2 t. salt
1 t. pepper, freshly ground
4 bay leaves
1 c. brown sugar
1 c. white wine

In large bowl, combine chicken with prunes, olives, capers, vinegar, olive oil, oregano, garlic, salt, pepper, and bay leaves. Mix well. Cover and marinate in refrigerator overnight. Place chicken in single layer in shallow baking pan. Spoon marinade over chicken. Sprinkle chicken with brown sugar and pour in wine. Bake in pre-heated 350 degree oven for 1 hour.

Place chicken on platter with prunes, olives, and capers. Marinade may be thickened with flour and served on the side. This recipe also works well with comparable weight of chicken steaks for a larger group.

Serves 6.

Rev. Ron Gollatz

Chicken Bernardin

1/4 c. salt pork, finely diced
1 (3-1/2 lb.) frying chicken
2 T. butter
1/4 c. vegetable oil
2 leeks
20 shallots or small onions
salt, to taste
white pepper to taste
1 clove garlic, pressed
3 T. parsley, freshly minced
3/4 c. sweet white wine
3/4 c. chicken broth
1/2 c. whipping cream
1 (5 oz.) can black or button mushrooms
      or 1 lb. of fresh mushrooms

Soak pork in enough water to cover for 30 minutes. Drain well.. Cut chicken into serving pieces. Remove skin.

Melt 1 T. butter with 1/4 c. oil in a large heavy skillet over medium heat. Add chicken. Sauté on all sides until lightly browned. Drain off the excess fat and set aside.

Trim off and discard the green end from the leeks. Cut the white part into thin slices. Combine pork, leeks, and shallots in a saucepan over medium heat. Cook, stirring constantly, until lightly browned. Add to the chicken. Add salt, pepper, garlic, parsley, wine, and broth. Cover and simmer about 45 minutes or until chicken is tender. Remove chicken, pork, and vegetables with slotted spoon. Place on heated serving platter. Keep warm.

Add cream to the liquid in the skillet. Simmer until the liquid is of sauce consistency. Add half the mushrooms. Heat through.

Spoon sauce over chicken and vegetables. Border with rice. Garnish with remaining mushrooms which have been lightly sautéed in 1 T. butter.

Fresh mushrooms, cooked with pork mixture can be used instead of canned mushrooms. Remove from pork mixture after browned. Add to sauce same as for black mushrooms. Serves 6.

Joseph Cardinal Bernardin

Deep Fried Turkey

turkey
peanut oil
salt and cayenne pepper

Season a fresh, cleaned and dried small turkey inside and out with a combination of salt and cayenne pepper to taste. In a large deep-frying pot, heat peanut oil to 325 to 350 degrees. Carefully lower the whole turkey into oil, cavity side toward the top. Cook the turkey for 4 minutes per pound. Watch for spattering, and occasionally push the turkey down into the oil if it rises. This is a wonderful way to produce a moist, juicy turkey. Very different, and worth a try!

Rev. Jerry Williams, O. Carm.

Chicken Lasagna

8 oz. lasagna noodles
1 (10 oz.) can cream of mushroom soup, undiluted
2/3 c. milk *or* wine
1/2 t. salt
1/2 t. poultry seasoning
8 oz. cream cheese, softened
2 c. cream cottage cheese
2/3 c. stuffed olives, sliced
1/3 c. chopped onion
1/3 c. green pepper, chopped
1/3 c. parsley, minced
4 or 5 chicken breasts, cooked, skinned, and sliced
1-1/2 c. buttered bread crumbs

Cook noodles and rinse in cold water. Mix soup, milk (or wine), salt, and poultry seasoning and beat together. Beat the cheeses together and stir in olives, onion, green pepper, and parsley. Place half of noodles in a 8x12-inch baking dish. Spread with half the cheese, then half the chicken breast slices. Then half the soup mixture. Repeat layers, top with crumbs. Bake at 350 degrees for 45 minutes. Let stand for 10 minutes. Can be frozen.

Rev. Thomas S. Boyle

Chicken Paprika

1 (3 to 3-1/2 lb.) broiler-fryer chicken
1/4 c. olive oil or vegetable oil
1 large onion coarsely chopped
1 can (about 12 oz.) chicken broth
1 T. paprika
1 t. seasoned salt
fresh ground pepper
1/2 c. sour cream

In a large skillet heat oil and brown chicken over medium heat. Remove chicken. Add onion to skillet; sauté until translucent. Add chicken, broth, paprika, salt, and pepper to taste. (*You can also use your favorite tomato sauce from a jar.*) Cover and cook over medium heat for 30 to 40 minutes until tender. Remove chicken to serving platter or bowl and cover to keep warm. Stir sour cream into mixture in skillet and heat until warm. Pour over chicken and serve.

Rev. Ken Fleck

Chicken Steaks in Mustard/Caper Sauce

4 chicken steaks
2 T. flour
salt & pepper to taste
2 T. butter
1/2 c. dry white wine
juice from 1/2 lemon
1 T. Dijon mustard
2 T. capers, drained (more to taste)

Pound chicken steaks between 2 sheets of wax paper to uniform thickness. Mix flour with salt and pepper; dust both sides of chicken with seasoned flour. Melt butter in large skillet. Add chicken and cook on each side until nicely browned, about 4 to 5 minutes. If pan is crowded, cook in two batches. Remove chicken and keep warm. Add wine and lemon juice to pan. Cook and stir to scrape up browned bits. Stir in mustard and capers. Cook over high heat for 1-2 minutes. Pour over breasts and serve.

Serves 2-3.

Rev. Ron Gollatz

Coq au Vin
(Chicken in Red Wine)

There are many variations of this classic French dish. I first had it served by nuns at St. Bride's Parish. I later tried it in Paris with a stronger, deeply colored gravy only to learn that they use chicken blood in the recipe. I have decided to give you an altered version.

1/4 c. olive oil
1 large onion, diced large
3 cloves of garlic minced
1/2 lb. fresh, sliced mushrooms
6 slices of bacon
1 (3-1/2 – 4 lbs.) broiler-fryer chicken, cut up
      or 3 lbs. chicken breasts
1 bay leaf
1/2 t. dried thyme
parsley, snipped
2 T. brandy
1 c. **deep red wine** (Burgundy, Cabernet Sauvignon, Pinot Noir)
1 c. **beef consume** (or **1 c. water and 1 beef bouillon cube**)

Into a large skillet over medium-high heat, add olive oil, onions, and garlic. Sauté until tender. Add mushrooms. Sauté for a few minutes until tender. Remove to a separate bowl. Deglaze pan with a little red wine and pour over onions and mushrooms.

In the same pan, fry the bacon until crisp. Set bacon aside. In the fat still in the pan, brown the chicken. Drain off the fat. In the same pan with the chicken, add the onions, mushrooms, crumbled bacon, seasonings, wine, brandy, and broth. Cover and let simmer on low heat for 45 to 60 minutes until chicken is tender.

To thicken the gravy make a roux from 3 T. flour mixed into 3 T. melted butter in a small pan. Lightly brown the flour in the butter. Remove the chicken to a serving platter or bowl. Add the roux to the gravy in the skillet. Allow the gravy to thicken for a few minutes and pour over the chicken.

Serve over noodles or rice. Serves 4-6.

Rev. Ken Fleck

Everyday Meat Loaf

2 beaten eggs
3/4 c. milk
2/3 c. bread crumbs
2 T. grated onions
1 t. salt
dash of pepper
1-1/2 lbs. of ground meat

Combine eggs, milk, bread crumbs, onions, salt, and pepper. Add meat, and mix well. Pat mixture in loaf pan. Bake at 350 degrees for 1 hour 15 minutes.

Rev. Ken Fleck

Festive Roast Pork

2 3-lb. boneless loin roasts
4 Jonathan apples
2 large white onions
2 c. orange juice
Spices:
   pepper, seasoned salt, garlic powder, rubbed sage,
   parsley flakes

Preheat oven to 325 degrees. Wash meat under cold water. Pat dry. Generously season both pork loins with above spices. Place one loin in 9x13 inch roasting pan. Place three thinly sliced wedges of onion on top of first roast. Secure with skewers or string. Repeat with second roast. Pour orange juice around meat. Quarter and core apples, unpeeled, and place in juice around roasts. Chunk onions and place around roasts with apples and orange juice. Roast uncovered for 00 min. or until internal temperature reads 160 degrees. Remove roasts and place on platter. Cover with foil and allow to rest for 15 min. before carving. Surround with fresh parsley and a jar of spiced apples.

Gravy:

After removing roasts from pan, pour contents of pan into blender, including onions and apples. Puree. Reheat in microwave, if necessary. Serve gravy over Pepperidge Farm apple, raisin, and cinnamon stuffing. Serve with favorite green vegetable.

Rev. Gene Burns

Flemish Beef Carbonnade

3 slices smoked bacon
3 large onions, peeled
2 T. brown sugar
2 T. red wine vinegar
salt and pepper to taste
1 T. vegetable oil
2 lbs. lean beef (for stew) cut into 1 in. cubes
1/4 c. all-purpose flour
12 oz. dark beer
1 bay leaf
3/4 t. dried thyme

Brown bacon in a Dutch oven or 4 qt. oven-safe casserole dish. Remove bacon and slice onions thinly. Add onions to bacon drippings and simmer until limp (about 20 minutes).

Add sugar and increase to medium heat. Stir often until onions become golden brown (7-9 minutes). Add vinegar, salt, pepper. Mix well and set aside in a bowl.

Heat oven to 350 degrees. Add oil to Dutch oven or casserole bowl; heat. Add meat in batches. Brown meat on all sides. Put all meat in Dutch oven or casserole; sprinkle with flour and mix. Add beer, bay leaf, and thyme. Heat to boil. Add onions and bacon. Remove from heat. Mix. Bake covered, in oven until meat is tender (1 to 1-1/2 hrs.). Serve with rice, potatoes, or noodles.

Rev. Bill O'Connor
Rev. Ben Guirsch

Turkey Casserole

1 lb. uncooked ground turkey
1 can (15 oz.) mixed vegetables
1 can condensed cream of chicken soup
Tater Tots *or* small carrots

Stir all ingredients together and spoon into casserole dish. Top with tater tots (or small carrots). Bake at 375 degrees for 1 hour. Serves 3.

Rev. Bruce Wellems, CMF

Flynn's Chicken Casserole

1 pkg. (12 oz.) chicken stove top stuffing
2 pkg. stove top seasoning
1 c. water
3/4 c. butter
2-1/2 c. cooked chicken, cut up in pieces (3 single breasts)
1/2 c. chopped onions
1/2 c. chopped celery
3/4 c. mayonnaise
3/4 t. salt
2 eggs
1-1/2 c. milk
1 can (13 oz.) chicken broth
2 c. grated mozzarella cheese

Make stuffing according to package directions, using the stuffing mix, 2 pkgs. seasoning, water, and butter.

Place half of the stuffing mix in the bottom of a greased pan. Mix chicken, onion, celery, mayonnaise, and salt. Spread over the bottom layer of stuffing. Cover with remaining stuffing. Beat eggs and milk together and pour over the casserole. Cover and refrigerate overnight.

When ready to cook, pour chicken broth over the casserole. Bake, uncovered at 350 degrees for 40 to 50 minutes. Remove from oven, grate mozzarella cheese over the top and return to oven for 5 minutes to melt cheese.

Rev. Jerry Williams, O. Carm.

Pork Chop Bake for 12

12 pork chops
8 medium potatoes, peeled and sliced thinly
2 medium onions, sliced thinly
2 beef bouillon cubes
6 carrots, cut in thin sticks

Season pork chops with pepper and salt. Cut diagonal slices along edge of pork chops and broil until brown. Mix potatoes, onions and carrots in large casserole dish. Boil 2 cups of water and completely dissolve beef cubes. Arrange chops on vegetable mixture. Pour boiling beef cubes over all and cover. Bake at 350 degrees for 1 hour and 45 minutes.

Br. Leonard M. Lawrence

Gumbo

1/2 c. butter *or* vegetable oil
1 large onion, diced
3 cloves garlic, minced
1/2 c. flour
1 to 3 t. cayenne pepper (or to taste)
3 T. filé powder*
1 T. parsley, snipped
1 lb. ham, cubed
1 lb. hot sausage, sliced in cartwheels
3 lbs. chicken wings, tips cut off
2 c. oyster *or* clam juice *or* chicken stock
4 c. water
1 lb. shrimp, peeled and deveined

Fry the onions in the butter or oil until translucent. Add garlic and flour. Continue cooking over medium heat until flour is a chocolate brown. Be careful not to burn by stirring constantly. Add cayenne, filé powder and parsley. Fry smoked sausage and ham until heated.

In a large 5-6 qt. crock pot or large stew pot combine flour mixture, sausage, ham, and chicken, add broth and water to barely cover. Simmer over low heat on stove top for 2 hours or in crock pot for 4 to 6 hours on high (longer on low). Add cleaned shrimp just 10 minutes before serving. Serve over rice. Serves 8-12.

Rev. Ken Fleck

---

*Filé powder is made from sassafras leaves and is hard to find. The Choctaw Indians gave it to the French to thicken their gumbo.

Steak for 2

2 steaks

Broil for 4 minutes on either side. Slowly sip martini as steaks cook. You're all set!!

Rev. Art Fagan

Honey Mustard Salmon

2 to 3 lbs. salmon fillets
1/2 c. favorite honey mustard salad dressing
1 t. dry mustard
1 to 2 T. turmeric

Clean and pat dry the fillets. Place on a lightly greased cookie sheet.

Mix the turmeric, dry mustard, and your favorite dressing. Coat the fillets generously, leaving about 1/2 inch from the edge. Broil six inches from source of heat for approximately 10 minutes.

Keep some sauce in reserve for additions after the fish is finished cooking.

To make sharper, add 1 to 2 T. Dijon mustard.

Rev. Ken Fleck

Ken's Italian Chicken

1 roasting chicken, cut into parts
6 small, new potatoes
1 jar medium to hot Italian Peperoncíni, with juice
3 small yellow onions
2 garlic cloves, minced
1/2 c. olive oil

Place chicken in a 9x13 inch roasting pan. Scrub the potatoes and peel, leaving a narrow band of skin around the middle of the potato. Arrange around the chicken. Peel the onions, and cut in half. Arrange with chicken and potatoes. Pour Peperoncíni, juice and all over the chicken. Mix minced garlic with the olive oil and pour over the chicken. Cover with foil and bake at 350 degrees for 1 hour. Remove foil, baste with juices, return to oven uncovered for browning. This is a nicely spiced, slightly hot dish, served well with a pasta.

Rev. Jerry Williams, O. Carm.

Meat Loaf

2 lbs. ground beef
1 egg
1 c. onion diced small
3/4 c. dry breadcrumbs
4 oz. tomato sauce
1 t. Mrs. Dash
1 t. Liquid Smoke
1 t. Worcestershire sauce
1/2 t. dry mustard
1/4 t. fresh ground pepper

Mix all ingredients in a large bowl. In a casserole dish form your meat loaf. Bake at 350 degrees for 60 minutes.

Basics to creative meat loaf:

The first four ingredients are the basics to making good meat loaf. The rest is up to your imagination depending on what direction you want to go. Be creative!!!

Italian Meat Loaf: Add tomato paste, Italian seasonings, oregano, salt, and garlic, to taste.

Oriental Meat Loaf: Add soy sauce, Teriyaki Sauce, mushrooms, bean sprouts, garnish with rice noodles or chow mein noodles.

Mexican Meat Loaf: Add crushed red pepper or cayenne, hot sauce, chili powder, Jalapenos.

You get the idea...Be creative!..Experiment!

Rev. Ken Fleck

Oven-Baked Chicken

Chicken pieces (with skin, or skinless)
1 container (8 oz.) of frozen orange juice concentrate
1 pkg. dried French onion soup mix

Clean and prepare chicken and place in greased pan. Mix frozen orange juice concentrate with the onion soup mix. Spread on top of the chicken pieces. Place in oven uncovered for one hour at 350 degrees. Enjoy!

Rev. James J. Close

Lentenburgers

2 (6 oz.) cans of tuna, drained and flaked
3 T. mayonnaise or salad dressing
1/2 c. chopped celery
dash of celery salt
4 hamburger buns (split)
8 slices mozzarella or American cheese
8 slices tomato (optional)

Mix tuna, mayonnaise, celery, and celery salt. Place on bun halves. Add a slice of cheese and broil until golden and bubbly. Top with tomato.

Rev. Leon R. Wagner

Merle's Sausage Jambalaya

1 T. vegetable oil
1 medium onion, diced
1/4 c. green pepper, diced
1 large celery stalk, diced
2 c. rice, uncooked and unwashed
2 cans (10-1/2oz.) beef consommé
1 can water
2 T. stick margarine
1 t. thyme
1 t. garlic powder
1 t. salt
1 lb. smoked sausage, sliced thinly

In a large skillet over medium heat add oil, onion, green pepper, and celery. Sauté until tender crisp, about 5 minutes. Add sausage and continue cooking for another 5 minutes.

In an oven-safe casserole dish or a small roasting pan place rice, consommé, water, margarine, and seasonings. Bake at 375 degrees for 30 minutes. Stir well, add sautéed veggies and sausage, return to oven for 55 minutes. Serves 6-8

Rev. Ken Fleck

My Chicken

6 single chicken breasts
2 cloves garlic, minced
1/2 c. soy sauce
1/2 c. water
salt and pepper to taste
1/2 stick butter
paprika

Place chicken, skin side up in a 9x13-inch pan. Mix garlic, soy sauce, water, salt, and pepper together and pour over the chicken. Bake at low heat, 250 degrees for 1/2 hour. Turn chicken skin side down and return to oven for 1/2 hour. Turn chicken skin side up, baste with juices, dot with butter and sprinkle with paprika and return to oven till nicely browned. Great with rice, serve juice slightly thickened with cornstarch as a gravy.

Rev. Jerry Williams, O. Carm.

Oriental Oven Pork (OOPs)

6 double thick pork chops

<u>Coating</u>:
1 egg
3 t. soy sauce
1 T. sherry *or* Madeira
1/8 t. ground ginger
2 cloves crushed garlic *or* 1/2 t. garlic powder
1/2 c. breadcrumbs

Spray oven baking dish with vegetable shortening. Beat egg, soy sauce, sherry, ginger, and garlic. Dip chops in coating mixture then in breadcrumbs. Arrange in a single layer in the pan. Bake at 350 degrees for 30 minutes. Turn chops over and bake another 20 minutes. Serves 6.

Rev. Ken Fleck

Pepper Steak

3 lbs. of round steak
2 green bell peppers
2 T. cooking oil
1 clove garlic, minced
1 t. salt
1 med. ginger, diced
1/3 c. soy sauce
1 pkg. of au jus gravy

Cut beef thin and long. Do the same with the bell peppers.

Sauté garlic in oil until brown. Add the cut beef and cook until brown. Add salt, ginger, and soy sauce to taste as desired. Do not over cook beef, do not add water. Put on low heat then add peppers and au jus gravy. Mix well. Serve nice and hot.

Rev. Jack Farry
by Gisele Derose

Roast Beef Salad

2 lbs. roast beef cut into strips
    (regular thick cut beef from the deli)
4 shallots, minced
1 pkg. (20 oz.) frozen peas, thawed
1/4 c. parsley
1/2 c. fresh lemon juice
1-1/2 T. red wine vinegar
1/4 c. mustard
1 clove garlic, minced
1/2 t. salt
fresh ground pepper to taste
1/2 c. vegetable oil
Possibly add beets, mushrooms, or carrots for color only.

In a large bowl combine all ingredients. Mix well. Serve at room temperature.

Rev. Daniel P. Coughlin

Pollo Arrosto All'Aglio e Rosmarino
Roast Chicken with Oil and Rosemary

1 (3-1/2 lb.) chicken, cleaned and dry
2 cloves garlic, unpeeled and crushed
1 sprig fresh (or 1 t. dried) rosemary
salt and pepper
1 T. olive oil
1 T. butter, softened
rosemary sprigs for garnish

Preheat oven to 450 degrees. Put the garlic and rosemary in the chicken's cavity and sprinkle cavity with salt and pepper. Truss the bird. Rub the skin of the chicken with butter and olive oil and season with more salt and pepper. Roast chicken on a rack, brushing with pan juices, 20-25 minutes until golden brown. Lower oven temperature to 375 degrees and roast chicken, basting frequently with pan juices, for 30 to 35 minutes, or until the juices run clear. Let the chicken rest, loosely covered with foil, for 10 minutes. Remove the trussing strings. Garnish with rosemary and serve with pan juices. Serves 4-6.

In case you're wondering how a German got these Italian dish - es, I've lived and worked in Assisi the past 8 years. These are my favorites, outside of breads and pastas. Buon appetito!

Rev. Robert Hutmacher, OFM

Turkey Steaks with Basil and Mustard

1/4 c. olive oil
1 T. Worcestershire sauce
2 t. Dijon mustard
1 t. dried basil
4 turkey steaks *or* chicken steaks, pounded to uniform thickness
1 red pepper, diced

Mix oil, Worcestershire sauce, mustard, and basil. Heat in large skillet over medium-high heat. Add turkey and red pepper, cover and cook 3 minutes. Turn, cover and continue cooking until done, and no longer pink, about 3 minutes. Serve with red peppers spooned over. Serves 4.

Rev. Ron Gollatz

Salmon Cheese Soufflé

1/4 c. butter
1/4 c. flour
1 c. milk
1/4 t. salt
4 oz. shredded American cheese
1 small can (12-15 oz.) red or pink salmon
4 eggs

Melt butter in sauce pan over medium heat. Add flour and stir until blended. Stir in milk and salt. Cook until thickened. Add cheese and stir until smooth. Remove from heat. Add salmon. Mix well. Allow to cool while preparing eggs.

Separate yolks from egg whites. Add beaten egg yolks to mixture. Beat egg whites until stiff peaks form. Fold stiffly beaten egg whites into mixture. Spray casserole dish with vegetable shortening. Pour mixture into dish. Set dish in a pan of hot water.

Bake in a preheated oven 350 degrees for 60 minutes. Serves 4.

Rev. Ken Fleck

Spanish Pot Roast

3 to 4 lb. pot roast
8 oz. bottle Catalina dressing
1/2 c. water
1 c. sliced green olives (salad olives)
8 small onions or large onion, cut into eighths
8 small potatoes

Brown meat slowly in 1/4 c. dressing. Add remaining dressing and water; cover and cook slowly (med. low heat) for 2 to 2-1/2 hours. Add olives, onions, and potatoes; cook 45 minutes or until meat and vegetables are tender. Serves 6 to 8.

Rev. Ron Gollatz

Deviled Chicken

3 lbs. boneless chicken breasts
1/2 c. olive oil
1/4 c. lemon juice
2 t. Dijon mustard
1 t. Tabasco sauce
1/2 t. salt
1/2 t. fresh ground pepper
1 T. fresh rosemary
1/4 t. hot dry chili flakes

Separate the chicken breasts into individual pieces. Mix all of the ingredients into a large bowl. Place the chicken breasts into the bowl and let them marinate overnight. BBQ the breasts on the grill 4 minutes per side. Or bake at 350 degrees for 15 minutes. Serve with the spaghetti described below.

Rev. Larry Lisowski

Spaghetti in Aïoli Sauce

1/2 lb. spaghetti
1 c. olive oil
3 cloves garlic, chopped

Prepare the spaghetti. Heat oil in small pan. Add 3 cloves of chopped garlic. Warm but do not burn the garlic. Garlic will turn brown, but do not let them turn black. Mix the oil and garlic into the spaghetti and serve with the chicken.

Rev. Larry Lisowski

Swedish Meatballs

1 bottle Heinz chili sauce
1 jar Smucker's grape jam

Make any meatloaf recipe. Make small balls and place on cookie sheet and bake at 375 degrees for 10 minutes.

Take one bottle of Heinz chili sauce and one bottle of Smucker's grape jam and melt together. Place meatballs and sauce in fondue pot. Heat and serve and ENJOY!!!

Rev. Edwin Bohula (Capt., CHC, USN, Ret.)

Southern Chicken and Rice

8-10 pieces of cut up chicken
1 c. flour
white pepper
salt
garlic powder
chopped celery, as needed
chopped onion, as needed
chopped red bell pepper, as needed
1/2 stick butter
1 can (14 oz.) chicken broth

Flour chicken in 1 cup of flour with white pepper, salt, garlic powder. Brown on both sides. Lay chicken in long baking dish. Cover with chopped celery, onion, and a bit of red bell pepper. Dot with 1/2 stick of butter. Sprinkle a little flour over chicken and pour 1/2 can of chicken broth over. Cover with foil or lid. Bake at 350 degrees for 30 minutes or until chicken is tender. Serve with cooked rice. Make sure there is some gravy.

Rev. Howard Tuite
by Mrs. Christine Radford

Steak San Marco

2 lb. chuck roast, cut in strips and trim off large hunks of fat
1 pkg. Lipton onion soup mix
2 cloves of fresh garlic (use garlic press)
1 t. oregano
pepper
2 T. Heinz wine vinegar
2 T. olive oil
1 can (28 oz.) Italian tomatoes

Put meat in pot on top of stove and add all the additional ingredients. Let cook over medium heat 3 to 3-1/2 hours. Serve with medium buttered noodles. Serves 6.

Rev. Ken Fleck

Sephardic Chicken

1 chicken, cut up (4 lbs. or so)
1 lemon, cut into wedges
garlic powder
1/2 c. olive oil
1/4 c. vinegar
1/4 c. sweet white wine
1 lb. small white onions
1/2 c. green olives
1/4 c. raisins
1 whole head of garlic
2 cloves
1 cinnamon stick
2 bay leaves
1 T. peppercorns

Wash chicken pieces; rub with lemon. Sprinkle with garlic powder. Heat the olive oil in a large pot with lid. Brown the chicken pieces on all sides. Add oil, vinegar, and wine. Add the onions, olives, and raisins on top of chicken. Slice the top from the whole garlic head. Put the garlic in the middle of the pot. Sprinkle the cut pieces in the pot with the rest of the spices. Cover and simmer over low heat for about one hour. Serve with potatoes, rice, or noodles.

Rev. Bill O'Connor
Rev. Ben Guirsch

Pork Chops Abracadabra

2 to 4 pork chops (with or without bone); thick is better
1 can (10-1/2 oz.) Campbell's condensed soup
      (cream of mushroom, broccoli, celery, etc.)
1 T. dried minced onion (optional)

Pour the contents of the soup can into a slow cooker (do NOT add water or milk). Arrange the pork chops on top of the soup and cook at medium heat for 4-5 hours. Minced onions may be added at any time up to an hour before serving.

This recipe is the lazy pastor's answer to starvation. The recipe in not an original, but it's delicious and EASY!

Rev. John P. Finnegan

Vegetarian Chili Mac

1 pkg. (7-8oz.) favorite macaroni & cheese
1 can (15 oz.) hot chili beans in sauce
1 medium onion, coarsely chopped
2 T. vegetable oil
1 T. chili powder
1 t. crushed red pepper
1 medium green bell pepper, chopped
1 medium red bell pepper, chopped

Prepare macaroni & cheese according to directions on package. Sauté onion in a nonstick frying pan with the oil over medium heat until translucent. Add chili beans and sauce to onions. Mix in chili powder, crushed red pepper. Cook for 5 minutes. Add chopped red and green peppers and turn off heat. Finish preparing the macaroni and cheese.

Serve in bowls with macaroni placed on bottom, a scoop of the chili mixture placed in the center. Garnish with either a light sprinkling of paprika on the macaroni or hickory flavored barbecue sauce. Serves 4-6.

Rev. Ken Fleck

Argentine "Mondongo" (Tripe and Chickpeas)

1-1/2 cups chickpeas
2 large onions, sliced thin
1 Spanish sausage (red)
1-1/2 lbs. prepared tripe
1 small can tomatoes
3 cloves garlic, optional
Spanish ground red pepper
salt

Soak chickpeas over-night in water. Cook onions in olive oil with the sausage cut into thin slices until slightly brown, then add all other ingredients with water to cover and cook until peas are tender. If one cannot get the sausage, one might add a little pork/pork bones or both.

Rev. Christopher Gibson, CP

Argentine Vegetable "Cannelloni"

Dough:
>   5 c. flour
>   2 eggs
>   1 t. salt
>   3/4 c. cold water
>   grated cheese

Put the flour on a board and make a well in the center. Into this, put the eggs, salt, and enough water to make a dough, which is not too hard and not too soft. Roll the dough very thin and cut into squares of 4x4 inches. Cook them in hot salted water. Drain and place them on a board that has been sprinkled with grated cheese.

Filling:
5 T. oil
1 choice garlic, chopped
1 onion, finely chopped
3 bunches Swiss chard, cooked
6 bunches spinach, cooked
1/2 c. cooked ham, chopped
1/2 c. fresh soft bread crumbs, moistened in milk
1 T. parsley, chopped
1 egg
salt, pepper, and nutmeg
tomato and meat sauces
grated cheese

Heat the oil in a large saucepan and fry the onion and garlic until golden brown, then add the rest of the ingredients. Mix well.

Cover the bottom of an oblong oven dish with tomato and meat sauces Place the prepared filling on the cannelloni squares, roll them and place them close to each other in the oblong oven dish. Cover the cannelloni with the same sauce and sprinkle them with grated cheese and finish cooking them in a very hot oven for about 15 minutes.

Rev. Christopher Gibson, CP

Portuguese Style Chicken

2 T. olive oil
1 c. red bell pepper, sliced
1 c. green bell pepper, sliced
1 c. yellow bell pepper, sliced
1 c. sliced onion
1 T. garlic, minced
salt
pepper
1 c. crushed tomatoes, canned
1/4 t. saffron *or* 1/2 t. turmeric
2 T. butter
4 chicken breasts, (1-1/4 lb.)
1 T. shallots, chopped
1/4 c. dry white wine
1/4 c. chicken broth
4 T. parsley, chopped

Heat the oil over medium high heat in a skillet. Add peppers, onions, garlic, salt and pepper. Cook, stirring until crisp-tender, about 3 minutes. Then add tomatoes and saffron or turmeric. Cover and simmer for 10 minutes.

Meanwhile, melt the butter in a skillet large enough to hold chicken breasts in one layer. Season the chicken with salt and pepper. Cook over medium heat until lightly browned, about 4 minutes. Turn the pieces, reduce the heat and cook until done, about 5 minutes. Do not overcook. Transfer the chicken to a warm platter and keep it warm. Add the shallots to the skillet and cook until wilted. Do not brown. Pour in the wine and scrape the bottom with a wooden spatula to dissolve any brown particles that may cling to the bottom of the skillet. Reduce the wine almost completely and add the chicken broth. Let this cook until it is almost totally reduced. Add the chicken breasts and any liquid that may have accumulated. Add the pepper and tomato mixture, bring to a simmer and add parsley. Serve with rice.

Rev. Thomas M. Enright

Chicken and Rice Casserole

1 c. brown rice
2 T. corn oil margarine
6 T. flour
1-1/2 c. chicken stock
1 c. milk
1 t. salt
1/8 t. garlic powder
1/8 t. freshly ground pepper
1/2 c. mushrooms, sliced or pieces
1 c. onion, chopped
1/2 t. onion powder
2 c. water
4 chicken breasts, skinned and halved

Heat oven to 350 degrees. Line a 9x13 inch baking dish with foil. Pour in rice to cover bottom. Melt margarine in heavy skillet over medium heat. Add flour. Cook and stir 1 minute. Do not brown! Add chicken stock and milk. Using wire whisk, stir the mixture over medium heat until it comes to a boil. Add salt, garlic powder, pepper, and mushrooms. Continue to cook for 1 minute more. Remove from heat and stir in onion, onion powder, and water. Pour half soup mixture over rice. Lay skinned and split chicken breasts on top and pour remaining soup over chicken. Bake uncovered, 1 hour or till chicken is tener and no longer pink and rice is tender..

Rev. Thomas M. Enright

Ground Beef Surprise

1-1/4 lbs. of ground beef
1 can mushrooms
1 can Durkee's French Fried Onions
2 pkgs. frozen potato puffs
1 chicken bouillon cube

Line a casserole dish with the ground beef. Add the mushrooms, onions, and potato puffs, then pour the chicken bullion over all the other ingredients. Bake at 350 degrees for 1 hour.

Rev. Fran Ernst

Peanut Soup

1 lb. peanuts, skinned

1 medium onion, chopped

1 c. chopped celery

2 - 12oz cans chicken or vegetable stock

2 c. milk

2 T. butter

2 T. flour

1/4 c. cream

salt and pepper to taste

Place the nuts, onion and celery in a sauce pan. Simmer for one hour. Puree in a food processor. Melt the butter in a sauce pan. Add flour to make a roux. Cook for a few minutes, but do not let it brown. Add the stock and bring to a boil stirring constantly. The roux will thicken the mixture after it boils. Add the milk and nut mixture. Bring to a boil stirring occasionally. Before serving add cream. Add salt and pepper to taste. If using salted nuts you may not need to add any seasoning.

Fr. Ken Fleck

Parmesan Crumbed Drumsticks and Thighs

1/2 c. freshly grated Parmesan cheese
1/3 c. fine bread crumbs
1 garlic clove, minced
2 t. fresh lemon rind
1-2 t. salt
1 t. dried rosemary *or* 2 t. fresh rosemary
1 t. freshly ground pepper
1/4 t. cayenne pepper
2-1/2 lbs. drumsticks and thighs, patted dry
1 stick butter, melted

In a wide bowl, combine all ingredients except drumsticks, thighs, and butter. Stir well until blended. One piece of chicken at a time, brush with melted butter and dredge in Parmesan mixture, coating completely. If any mixture is left over, pat over chicken. Chill, covered loosely on a jellyroll pan at least 1 hour or up to 24 hours. Arrange chicken in a lightly buttered roasting pan. Drizzle with remaining butter, if any, and bake in a preheated 425 degree oven for 30 minutes or until tender.

Archbishop Wilton D. Gregory
Archdiocese of Atlanta

Chimichurri
Argentine Barbecue Sauce

oregano, fresh
wine vinegar
head of garlic
water
rock salt
peppercorns (do not powder)

Chop up oregano and garlic well. Into an empty wine bottle add ingredients in proportions according to taste, e.g. a handful of rock salt. Approximately 1/3 of the bottle will be filled with wine and the rest 2/3 with water. Cut 3 "v"-shaped grooves lengthwise along the cork. Place the cork on the bottle. The grooves in the cork will allow the barbecue sauce to be added to the meat from time to time as it is cooking. It is best to let the sauce stand a few days before using. As the sauce is used, just add more spices to replenish.

Rev. Christopher Gibson, C.P.

Chicken Breast ala Ryan

2 (6-oz. each) boneless chicken breasts, washed
1 egg, beaten
1 T. seasoned flour
1 T. butter

<u>Sauce</u>:
>   8 oz. apple juice
>   1 t. cinnamon
>   1 t. sugar
>   cornstarch
>   1/2 c. apples, peeled and chopped

Place breast in flour then egg and sauté in butter till brown, about 3 minutes per side. Move chicken to oven safe dish. Boil sauce ingredients and thicken with cornstarch. Finish with 1/2 cup of fresh peeled, chopped apples. Pour over chicken. Finish cooking chicken in a 350 degree oven for 15-18 minutes. Serve with "Ryan's Rice Pilaf"

Rev. Joe Ryan

Ryan's Rice Pilaf

2 oz. chopped onion
2 oz. chopped carrot
2 oz. chopped celery
2 oz. chopped red bell pepper
4 oz. butter
4 oz. rice
8 oz. rich chicken stock
parsley, chopped

Sauté onion, carrots, celery, red bell pepper, and butter till tender. Then add 4 oz. rice and 8 oz. rich chicken stock. Bring to a boil and cook 20 minutes. Covered, until rice is tender. Add chopped parsley. Enjoy!

Rev. Joe Ryan

Argentine "Locro"

500 grams (1 lb.) frozen corn (or white corn for 'pozole')
200 grams (1/2 lb.) kidney beans (or other 'frijoles')
1 kg. (2 lbs.) stewing meat
1 kg. (2 lbs.) pork bones (optional)
1/2 small cabbage
3 sweet potatoes and/or 4 leeks
1 medium slice squash
3 fresh garlic sausages or 10 cloves of garlic
1-1/2 c. of water
salt to taste

Soak beans overnight. Cut up stewing meat and pork, removing all visible fat and sinews and simmer in a casserole for about 2 hours. Add rest of ingredients and cook for another hour. Add water as needed.

Sauce:
2 large onions, diced
4 green peppers, diced
2 hot chili peppers, diced
1 T. paprika
2 T. sugar
salt to taste
generous amount of corn oil

Simmer all the ingredients in the oil (covered), until tender. About 1-1/2 hours.

Rev. Christopher Gibson, C.P.

"Cook's Night Off" Goulash

1 lb. ground beef
1 Bermuda onion
1 small jar Open Pit sauce
1 green pepper (chopped)
1 pkg. taco chips

Brown the beef. Drain excess fat. Add onion, green pepper, and sauce. Cook 10 minutes. Serve over taco chips.

Rev. Leon R. Wagner

Bird in a Bag

First, THE BIRD! This can be any kind of fowl: chicken, turkey (whole or parts), goose, pheasant, duck etc. Pop it into a large plastic baking bag and place the bag in a baking pan. Savor with crushed garlic to taste, 2 heaping t. of dried sage, thyme, and rosemary. Also place within the bag your favorite veggies – potatoes, carrots, onions, celery, parsnips, turnips, ... whatever you like.

When you've stuffed all these wonderful things into the bag, put about 2-1/2 cups of dry white wine in the bag. Tie it closed and puncture the top of the bag *5-7* times with a knife or fork.

Bake in a 350 degree oven for 10 to 15 minutes per pound, depending on the size of the bird. Remove the bird from the oven, split the top of the bag to release the steam. After about 10 minutes, serve.

Rev. John P Finnegan

Chicken McLaughlin

<u>Single Recipe</u>
6 large chicken breasts, boned and split
salt
pepper
Accent
1/2 c. margarine
3 cans (10-1/2 oz. each) condensed cream of chicken soup
1-1/2 c. sherry, Taylor Pale Dry
3/4 c. water
1 can (10 oz.) water chestnuts, drained and sliced
1 can (6 oz.) mushrooms, small whole ones or large sliced ones
4 T. green pepper, chopped
1/2 t. thyme, crushed

<u>Double Recipe</u>
12 large chicken breasts, boned and split
salt
pepper
Accent
1 c. margarine
5 cans (10-1/2 oz. each) condensed cream of chicken soup
2-1/2 c. sherry, Taylor Pale Dry
1-1/4 c. water
2 cans (10 oz. each) water chestnuts, drained and sliced
2 cans (6 oz. each) mushrooms, small whole or large sliced ones
8 T. green pepper, chopped
1 t. thyme, crushed

Lightly season chicken with salt and pepper. Brown slowly in margarine.
Arrange chicken, skin side up, in casserole. Add thyme to margarine to
dissolve it. Stir in soup to drippings in skillet, slowly add sherry and water
stirring until smooth. Add water chestnuts, mushrooms, and green pepper;
heat to boiling. Pour over chicken. Cover with foil, bake at 350 degrees
for 45 minutes. Uncover and bake 15 minutes longer, or until chicken is
tender. Serve over rice, garnish with spiced peaches if desired.

Rev. Edward McLaughlin

Easy Chicken Pot Pie

1 can (12-1/2 oz.) chicken meat
1 can peas
1 can carrots
1 can sliced potatoes
1 small onion, chopped
1 can (10-1/2 oz.) condensed cream of chicken soup
1/2 can (12 oz.) condensed milk
1 tube refrigerated biscuits
salt and pepper to taste

Drain vegetables and chicken. Mix above with cream of chicken soup and 1/2 can of milk. Place in a casserole dish; bake at 350 degrees for 30 minutes. Top with refrigerated biscuits and bake for 10 to 15 minutes.

Rev. Bernard Kennedy, OFM

Easy Lasagna

1 lb. ground beef
2 cloves garlic, crushed
1 can (6 oz.) tomato paste
1 can (1 lb. 4 oz.) tomatoes
1 t. salt
3/4 t. pepper
1/2 t. oregano
1/2 c. red wine
1-1/2 c. Mozzarella cheese, grated
24 oz. cream cottage cheese
1 package (8 oz.) lasagna noodles
Parmesan cheese, grated

Brown ground beef and garlic in a small amount of fat. (May also add onions to browning.) Add tomato paste, tomatoes, salt, pepper, oregano, and wine. Cover and simmer for 20 minutes. Cook noodles as directed on the package. Preheat oven to 350 degrees. Combine Mozzarella and cottage cheese. Alternate layers of meat, noodles, and cheese in a 12x8x2 inch baking dish, beginning and ending with meat sauce. Bake 20 to 30 minutes. Sprinkle with Parmesan cheese. Serves 6-8.

Rev. Ken Fleck

Flank Steak in Tangy Sauce

1-1/2 lb. flank steak
1/4 c. flour
1 t. salt
pepper to taste
2 T. shortening
1-1/2 c. water
1/2 c. catsup
1-1/2 T. prepared mustard
2 T. lemon juice
1/4 c. minced onion

Score meat. Mix flour, salt, and pepper. Thoroughly pound the mixture into the steak. Brown well in 2 T. hot fat. Combine the remaining ingredients; pour over the meat; cover and cook over low heat or in a slow oven until tender (about 1-1/2 to 2 hours). Serve surrounded by a border of fluffy rice. Garnish with parsley.

Rev. William H. Sheridan

Miller's Chicken

2 chicken breasts, boneless, skinless, diced into chunks
3 to 4 T. ketchup
3 to 4 T. honey
chopped garlic
dash of lemon juice
dash of Worcestershire sauce
chili powder
olive oil
chopped onion (optional)

Mix everything except chicken in a bowl. Heat a generous amount of olive oil, spoon the chicken and sauce into it. Cook. Flip frequently and keep it moving. When chicken is brown, turn down heat. Serve over rice, or on toothpicks with pineapple chunks as an appetizer or cook with potatoes and green peppers for a full meal.

Rev. Bob Miller

Stew for 6

1/2 onion, chopped
1/2 c. olive oil
5 to 6 garlic cloves, chopped
3 lbs. cubed meat (lamb, beef, chicken, etc.)
           coated in flour with salt and pepper to taste
8 oz. chicken broth
1/2 bunch of carrots, sliced and boiled until tender
6 oz. mushrooms, cut
4 oz. dry vermouth or Marsala

Heat cast iron pan. Add olive oil, onion and garlic. Reduce heat quickly to avoid burning. When they are translucent, add floured meat and brown lightly, add more oil if necessary. Keep stirring. Add chicken broth then carrots, mushrooms, and wine. Stir well. Place covered cast iron pan in a slow oven, about 250 degrees for 1–1/2 hours. Can be reduced to 200 degrees. Stir only occasionally. Serve with potatoes, or pasta, or rice.

Rev. Anthony Brankin

Baked Fillets in Sour Cream

lemon or onion, sliced thin
1 to 1-1/2 lb. fish fillets *or* 2 lb. fish steaks, 1 inch thick
2/3 c. sour cream
1/8 t. salt
pepper
paprika or dill

Start heating oven to 400°. Cover bottom of shallow baking dish with lemon (or onion) slices. Arrange fish on top. Sprinkle with some salt and pepper; cover and bake 00 minutes or until easily flaked with fork but still moist. Uncover and spread lightly with combined sour cream and salt; sprinkle with pepper and paprika. Place low in broiler until cream is lightly browned. Makes 4 servings.

Francis Cardinal George
by Sr. Mary Lucia

Sully's Spinach Lasagna

12 lasagna noodles,
   (cooked according to directions and cooled in water)
1/2 c. dried minced onion
2 packages (10 oz. each) frozen chopped spinach, thawed
1-1/2 c. dairy sour cream
1/2 t. salt
1 c. grated Parmesan cheese
1 T. flour
2 cans (8 oz. each) pizza sauce
1-1/2 c. shredded Mozzarella cheese

Preheat oven to 350 degrees. Combine onion, spinach, sour cream, salt, Parmesan cheese, and flour in a large bowl. Add 3/4 c. Mozzarella cheese to the mixture. Spread a small amount of pizza sauce on bottom of a 9x13 inch pan. Remove a lasagna noodle from the water, dry it thoroughly with a paper towel. Lay the noodle flat, put a large, rounded teaspoonful of the mixture near one end and roll it up jellyroll fashion. Place it in pan and repeat with remaining noodles. Cover with remaining sauce.

Cover with aluminum foil and bake for 30 minutes. Remove from oven, uncover, sprinkle with remaining Mozzarella, return to oven until cheese melts (about 15 minutes). Serves 6.

Rev. John D. Sullivan

Venetian Shrimp
Scampi alla Veneziana

1/2 c. extra virgin olive oil
2 T. minced garlic
2 t. fresh (*or* 1/2 t. dried) thyme
1/4 t. crushed hot red pepper
1 lb. large shrimp, shelled and deveined
salt
1/4 c. fresh parsley, snipped

In a large skillet heat the oil, garlic, thyme, and red pepper. Add the shrimp. Cook for about 5 minutes stirring constantly until all the shrimp are pink. Do not overcook. Shrimp get tough when overcooked! Transfer shrimp to a serving platter. Pour remaining sauce over them. Garnish with the parsley. Serve hot or cold. Serves 4 to 6.

Rev. Ken Fleck

Stuffed Turkey Breasts

6 turkey breasts, sliced
6 pieces of bacon
2 lbs. fresh asparagus
6 slices of Swiss cheese
6 slices of cooked ham
1 t. salt
1 t. pepper
1 t. garlic salt
1 t. onion salt
1 t. rosemary

Sauce:
    1 c. chicken broth
    2 cloves garlic
    2 bay leaves

Turkey breasts should be sliced thin (can be pounded), season each breast with seasonings. On each breast place one slice of ham, one slice of cheese and 4 stalks of asparagus (do not use tough ends). Roll up tight and wrap with bacon. Roll into flour and brown in oil. Place in baking dish with one cup chicken broth, 2 cloves garlic, and 2 bay leaves. Bake in covered dish at 350 degrees for 35 to 40 minutes. Serve with rice or noodles. Makes enough for 6.

Most Reverend Thomas G. Doran
Bishop of the Diocese of Rockford

Poached Nairobi Steak

1/4 c. corn oil
2 lbs. top round, cut into 1-inch cubes
3 to 4 medium onions, diced
12 oz. fresh mushrooms, sliced
1 c. malt vinegar
1 c. soy sauce

Into a large, deep skillet over medium high heat add your corn oil and sauté the beef cubes to seal in their juices. After about five minutes or when they are browned on all sides, add the remaining ingredients. Reduce the heat to low and simmer for 40 minutes. Serve with your favorite noodles. Serves 8.

Rev. Bill Knipe, Maryknoll Frs.

Will Burgers

ground round steak or ground chuck
seasoned salt
pepper, garlic, Worcestershire sauce
Parmesan cheese, grated

Season the ground meat to taste with salt, pepper, and garlic. Shape into patties for grill or broiler. Cook first side. After turning, pour Worcestershire sauce over the top and sprinkle with Parmesan cheese.

When done, serve. Take one bite before adding other condiments.

Rev. Bill Stenzel

Presto Chicken

I use Presto Kitchen Cooker which allows me to brown on high and then cook at a preset temperature.

12 chicken thighs, skinned, deboned, fat removed
Creole seasoning
1 or 2 T. butter, as needed
1 onion, chopped
1 clove garlic, minced
1 can (10-1/2 oz.) Campbell's cream of celery soup
1/2 c. dry white wine
juice of 1 lemon
1 can artichoke hearts (whole or halved), rinsed

Skin the chicken thighs, trim off the fat, and remove the bones. Season the meat with Creole seasoning. Set the cooker on high and brown the meat in butter. Add chopped onion and minced garlic.

When meat is browned, turn the cooker to 225 degrees. Spoon the soup over the meat. Rinse the can with 1/2 c. white wine and add to the meat. Squeeze in the juice of 1 lemon. Add the artichoke hearts. Cook at 225 degrees for 45 minutes.

Serves 4.

On special occasions I substitute a pork tenderloin.

Rev. Herb Myer

Tuna Noodle Dinner

1 pkg. medium or large egg noodles
1 can (10-1/2 oz.) cream of mushroom soup
1/2 soup can milk
1 small can peas, drained
1 small can mushroom pieces and stems, drained
1 egg, hard boiled and chopped
salt and pepper

Prepare the noodles according to directions.

In a saucepan heat the mushroom soup and milk until warm. Add the tuna, peas, mushroom pieces, and egg. Salt and pepper to taste. Heat and serve over a bed of egg noodles.

Rev. Paul Wachdorf

Chicken In Wine In No Time

1/2 c. flour
2 t. salt
1/2 t. pepper
2-1/2 to 3-1/2 lb. chicken, cut up
1 pkg. dry onion soup mix
1/4 c. oil
water
1 c. dry white wine

Combine flour, salt, pepper, and chicken in a paper bag. Shake bag to coat chicken pieces.

In a skillet brown the chicken pieces well on all sides in oil. Sprinkle with onion soup mix. Add the white wine and a little water. Cover and simmer about 45 minutes until tender. Serves 4.

Rev. David Cortesi

Notes

Angel Food

CAKE
MIX

Desserts

Apfelkuchen

1 egg
1/4 c. vegetable oil
1 c. milk
2 c. flour
1/2 c. sugar
1-1/2 t. baking powder
1/2 t. salt

In a large bowl beat together the egg, oil, and milk. Set aside.

Into another bowl sift together the flour, sugar, baking powder, and salt.

Combine the dry ingredients with the wet ingredients in the large bowl. Add 2 cups of your favorite fruit (blueberries, chocolate chips, dried fruit, diced apple pieces, etc.). Gently fold ingredients together until evenly moistened. Do not over mix.

Spoon batter into greased muffin tins or tins lined with paper. Bake at 400 degrees for 22-25 minutes. Yield 12 muffins.

Options

To make a coffee cake, place batter in a greased 9x9 pan (or two smaller pans, e.g. two greased pie tins). Arrange fresh fruit on top of the batter (e.g. apple wedges about 1/2 inch thick. Sprinkle generously with cinnamon sugar). Bake at 375 degrees for 25-30 minutes. Fresh fruit is best. If using canned fruit, drain it well before placing on top of batter.

This can be made in a larger cookie sheet by doubling the ingredients. Bake at 375 degrees for 25-30 minutes.

For a little added flavor you can:

- Add 1 t. almond or vanilla or other extract to the liquid ingredients
- Dust with powdered sugar when cool before serving.
- Serve warm with ice cream. Cinnamon ice cream goes well with the apple topping.
- Use plums to top instead of apples and serve with a plum sauce
- Make a glaze using powdered sugar and your favorite liquor. Drizzle over the cake before serving or serve it on the side.

Rev. Ken Fleck

Apple Crisp

8 cooking apples, pared and sliced
1/2 c. sugar
1/4 c. water

Topping
1 c. flour
3/4 c. sugar
1 t. baking powder
1/2 t. salt
1 egg, slightly beaten
1/2 c. butter, melted

Combine apples, sugar, and water in a shallow 1-1/2 qt. baking dish. Sift flour, sugar, baking powder, and salt. Add egg with pastry blender or fingers. Sprinkle over apples. Drizzle melted butter over all. Bake in preheated oven at 350 degrees for 35 minutes.

Serve topped with whipped cream or vanilla ice cream.

Rev. Ken Fleck

Apple Crisp

5 to 6 apples, skinned and sliced
1 c. Bisquick
1 c. sugar
dash of salt
1 unbeaten egg
1/3 c. butter, melted
cinnamon

Place apples on the bottom of a 8x8-inch baking dish. Mix the Bisquick, sugar, salt, and egg and sprinkle over apples. Pour 1/3 c. melted butter over all. Sprinkle cinnamon over top and bake at 350 degrees for 30 to 40 minutes. Serve with ice cream or cream.

Rev. Jerry Williams, O. Carm.

Apple Dip

1 pkg. (8 oz.) cream cheese
3/4 c. brown sugar
1/4 c. powdered sugar
1 t. vanilla
1/2 c. chopped peanuts
apples, sliced

Mix and chill. To keep the apple slices from turning brown, keep them in pineapple juice.

Rev. Edmund J. Schreiber
by Shirley Tadevic

Apple Slices

2 c. sifted flour
1/2 t. salt
2/3 c. margarine
2 egg yolks
1 T. lemon juice
1/4 c. cold water
2 cans (16 oz. each) apple pie filling *or*
              2 lbs. fresh sliced apples
1 c. sugar
2 T. flour
1/2 t. cinnamon

Sift flour with salt and cut in margarine as for a pie crust. Mix yolks, lemon juice, and water and sprinkle over flour. Blend lightly and divide into two parts. Roll first part to fit the bottom of a 9x13-inch baking pan.

Arrange apples on top of dough. Sprinkle sugar, flour, and cinnamon on top of apples. Roll remaining dough to fit over the top. Cut steam vents in top of crust and bake at 400 degrees for 30 to 40 minutes.

Glaze while still warm with 1 c. powdered sugar mixed with 2 T. melted butter, 1/2 t. vanilla, and 2 T. milk.

Rev. Jerry Williams, O. Carm.

Applesauce Pie

1-1/2 c. strained applesauce
3 T. butter, melted
1 c. sugar
1/2 t. salt
3 T. lemon juice
1 t. grated lemon rind
4 eggs, slightly beaten
unbaked 9-inch pie shell

Beat all ingredients together thoroughly and pour into shell. Bake at 450 degrees for 15 minutes. Reduce heat to 275 degrees and bake for 1 hour or more. Done when golden brown and the consistency of custard.

Rev. Jerry Williams, O. Carm.

Creamy Peach Pie

1 can (6 oz.) evaporated milk
1 can (15 oz.)cling peaches
1-1/2 t. plain gelatin
1 package (3 oz.) cream cheese, softened
1/4 c. granulated sugar
2 t. lemon juice
1 graham cracker pie crust

Chill milk to ice cold. Drain peach slices, saving syrup. Save a few slices of peach for garnishing; dice the rest. Soften gelatin in 1/4 c. of peach syrup. Melt this over medium heat. Remove from heat. To gelatin mix, blend in softened cream cheese and sugar. In another bowl, whip chilled milk in bowl until fluffy. Add lemon juice to milk mixture, whip until stiff. Beat in cheese mixture <u>slowly</u>. Fold in drained diced peaches. Turn into chilled graham crust. Top with peach slices. Chill 3 hours.

Rev. Ken Fleck

Baked Alaska

Bake your favorite box cake mix according to direction on box in the round form for two layers suggested on the box. Allow to cool completely and remove from pans to a cooling rack. Cake must be cool to touch before proceeding.

Place cake layers on an ovenproof plate or in a Pyrex pie dish or on a small metal pizza pan. Place in freezer for 30 to 60 minutes. Allow 1/2 gallon of your favorite ice cream to soften for easy forming.

Remove cake from freezer. With a large spoon scoop ice cream in layers from container and place on top frozen cake to form a mound. Since it is softened you should be able to eliminate most air pockets. Place back in freezer loosely covered with aluminum foil until ready to serve. Can be prepared up to two days ahead of time.

Preheat the oven to 500 degrees. Prepare meringue (cf. "MERINGUE" recipe in this section.) Spread over ice cream mound evenly. Be sure to completely cover the cake and ice cream and seal the meringue to the plate or pan. Place in oven just before serving for about 3 minutes to brown meringue The warm meringue and cold ice cream gives this dessert its name.

Some variations:

Garnish with frozen green and red grape clusters dusted with powdered sugar.

Use vanilla ice cream and serve with Cherries Jubilee, chocolate sauce, or fudge sauce.

Serve with butter pecan ice cream over a base made from a brownie mix.

Use a chocolate cake mix base with pistachio ice cream and garnish with sliced strawberries or a warm strawberry sauce.

Rev. Ken Fleck

Beth's Best Vanilla Cookies

5-1/2 sticks butter
2-1/2 c. sugar
10 eggs
3 T. vanilla extract
3 t. almond extract
1-1/2 c. milk
6 t. baking powder
5 lbs. flour

Cream butter and sugar with a mixer. Separate out 4 egg whites from the eggs and set aside. Place remaining eggs and yolks in mixer with creamed mixture. Add vanilla extract, almond extract, and milk. When blended, transfer to a large bowl to mix in flour. Sift baking powder with first addition of flour. Gradually add the remaining flour until dough is stiff.

Roll dough into 3/4-inch diameter ropes. In creative ways place dough on cookie sheets, e.g. braided, pretzel knots, canes, bows, etc. Bake at 350 degrees for 14 to 16 minutes.

Icing

4 egg whites you reserved
3 t. almond extract
3 t. vanilla extract
1-1/2 c. powdered sugar

Beat egg whites and extracts in a small bowl with a fork. Gradually add the powdered sugar until blended and smooth. Glaze cookies lightly.

Rev. Ken Fleck

*Bless, O Lord, all those who cook
A recipe found in this book.
Let them find a sweet surprise
As they grow, svelte and wise!*

Irene Hayes
St. George Parish

Carol's Cheating Cheese Cake

Love cheese cake but hate the heavy feeling on the stomach and conscience? This is for you.

Crust
1 c. plus 2 T. (10 oz.) margarine
2 c. flour
2 T. sugar

Mix together and press into a 9x13x2-inch pan. Bake at 350 degrees for 20 to 30 minutes. Allow to cool.

Filling
2 packages (8 oz. each) cream cheese (room temp)
2 c. powdered sugar
2 pkg. Dream Whip *or* 1 (16 oz.) container nondairy whipped topping
2 t. vanilla

Cream softened cheese with a mixer. Blend in powdered sugar. Add vanilla. Prepare Dream Whip as directed on package and fold into cheese mixture. Pour into cooled crust. Chill for 2 hours or longer.

Topping Options: (choose one)
1 - 20 oz. can of your favorite pie filling, e.g. cherry, blueberry, apple, etc.

Fresh soft fruits in season—strawberries, bananas, kiwis, blueberries (If preparing ahead of time you may want to put a clear fruit glaze over the fresh fruit. Fruit glaze is available in most grocery stores in the baking section.)

Rev. Ken Fleck

Chaplain B's Carrot Cake

4 jumbo eggs, well beaten
4 jars Gerber 3rd carrots (yes, baby food)
2 c. sugar
1-1/2 cup oil
2 t. baking powder
2 t. baking soda
2 t. cinnamon
1/4 t. salt
3 c. sifted all-purpose flour
1 c. chopped nuts (walnut bits)

Beat eggs in a large bowl. Add carrots, then sugar, mixing well. Add oil and blend well. Add dry ingredients slowly, mixing well. Add nuts last. Pour into 10" tube pan greased with oil or Pam. Bake at 350 degrees for 1-1/4 hours or until done.

Cream Cheese Frosting:
1 (8 oz.) pkg. cream cheese
1 box powdered sugar
1 t. vanilla
1/2 to 1 stick butter (truly optional to use)

Soften cream cheese (and butter, if used). Add the vanilla and then gradually the sugar. Spread on the cake as desired.

I usually use one bowl for making this cake. I do double the amount of nuts sometimes. Also, there is more frosting than needed, so it can be saved and/or used on a smaller cake, which I also do. When moved, I pour some batter into an aluminum cake pan for a small one for the house and a big cake to go. Big cake is just not high.

Rev. Edwin Bohula (Capt., CHC, USN, Ret.)

Cheesecake Supreme

Crust
16 small graham crackers, crumbled fine
1/2 stick butter or margarine, softened
1 T. honey
1 T. flour

Mix all ingredients together in a bowl. Mix well with hands. Press into the bottom of a 10-inch spring-form pan.

Filling
2 pkg. (8 oz. each) cream cheese, softened
1/3 c. sugar
4 eggs
1 t. vanilla extract
1 med. size lemon, grated rind and juice

Grate the lemon rind and squeeze it for the juice. Blend with all ingredients until creamy and smooth. Pour into crust. Bake in preheated oven at 375 degrees for 25 minutes. Remove from oven and allow to cool while you make the topping.

Topping
2 c. sour cream
1/2 c. sugar
1 t. vanilla extract

Blend together, mix well. Pour over cheesecake. Return to the 375 degree oven for 5 to 8 minutes. Remove from oven. Wait 12 hours before serving. Remove from pan to serving dish. Garnish with fresh, sliced strawberries, blueberries, slivered almonds, grapes dusted with powdered sugar. May also be topped with thinly sliced peaches, kiwi fruit, etc. in different patterns.

Continued on next page

Cheesecake Supreme (Cont'd.)

Cheesecake Variations

1. Make the base from crushed chocolate or vanilla wafers instead of graham crackers.

2. Use crushed Oreo cookies for the base instead of graham crackers.

3. Filling variations:
   - Mix in chocolate chips
   - Mix in peanut butter chips using the chocolate base
   - Mix in pistachio pudding mix instead of vanilla extract with chocolate base
   - Mix in 1 t. green food coloring into the filling and 1 t. mint extract with the chocolate base

Rev. Ken Fleck

Cheese Cookies

1/2 c. sharp cheddar cheese, shredded
1 c. whole wheat flour
3 T. oil
1/4 t. salt
dash of cayenne pepper
3-4 T. milk
1/3 c. nuts, finely crushed (may keep whole)

Mix first 5 ingredients till crumbly, add milk and chopped nuts, if desired. Knead into a large ball. Roll into a log and refrigerate until cold. Slice into 1/2-inch rounds, place on greased cookie sheet and bake at 350 degrees for 20 minutes. If desired, place a whole nutmeat on top of cookie before baking, and press lightly into dough. Great to serve with drinks, etc.

Rev. Jerry Williams, O. Carm.

Cheese Cake

2 c. graham cracker crumbs
1/2 c. melted margarine
3 T. sugar

Mix crumbs with sugar and margarine. Press into 13x9-inch pan or 9-inch spring-form pan.

Filling
3 pkgs. (8 oz. each) cream cheese, softened
1-1/4 c. sugar
3 eggs
2 t. vanilla

Topping
2 c. (8 oz.) sour cream
1 t. vanilla
4 T. sugar

Blend well.

Mix cream cheese and sugar. Add eggs one at a time. Add vanilla. Pour into crust. Bake at 350 degrees for 30 minutes. Do not overbake! Let cool 10 minutes then spread with topping. Turn the oven up to 400 degrees. Bake for 10 minutes. Chill 4 to 5 hours or overnight. Freezes well.

Rev. Ken Fleck

Raisin Rum Sauce

Use this sauce over ice cream, cheesecake, pound cake, or fresh fruit. Be creative.

2 T. butter
1 c. sugar
2 T. rum
1/2 c. golden or dark raisins

Mix all ingredients in a small sauce pan and heat gently until sugar is dissolved. May be thinned with more rum.

Rev. Ken Fleck

Chocolate Cheese Cake

1 c. graham *or* **chocolate cookie crumbs**
3 T. sugar
3 T. butter, melted

Mix. Press onto bottom of 9-inch spring-form pan.

Filling

1 package (12 oz.) of semisweet chocolate bits
    (For white chocolate, a 12 oz. chunk, broken into small
        pieces or shaved)
2 pkgs. (8 oz. each) cream cheese, softened
2 eggs
3/4 c. flour
1 t. vanilla

Melt the chocolate and beat together with the remaining ingredients. Pour over the crust and bake at 350 degrees for 1 hour and 15 minutes. Cool completely and garnish with whipped cream, cherries, and mandarin orange sections. You can make this into a swirl cake by using half white and half dark chocolate.

Rev. Jerry Williams, O. Carm.

Chocolate Pecan Pie

2 squares unsweetened chocolate
3 T. butter
3/4 c. sugar
1 c. light corn syrup
3 eggs, beaten slightly
1 t. vanilla
1 c. pecans
1 unbaked 9-inch pie shell

Melt first chocolate and butter together. Set aside. Combine sugar and corn syrup. Bring to quick boil. Boil 2 minutes. Add second mixture to chocolate mixture. Allow to cool 15 minutes. Pour slowly over eggs, stirring constantly. Add pecans and vanilla. Pour into unbaked pie shell and bake at 375 degrees for 45 to 50 minutes.

Rev. Jeffrey S. Grob

Cream Puffs

1 c. water
1 stick butter
1 c. flour
1/4 t. salt
4 eggs

In a small sauce pan bring water to a boil, add butter just to melt. Add flour and salt stirring constantly while still cooking until mixture forms a ball. Remove from heat and allow to cool slightly so that you can handle it. Add eggs one at a time beating vigorously after each addition. Drop by table-spoons onto a well-greased cookie sheet. Bake in a preheated oven at 400 degrees for 30 to 35 minutes or until golden brown. Allow to cool slowly. Cut off tops with a sharp knife and fill with your favorite whipped topping and fresh fruit. Garnish with dusting of powdered sugar or icing.

Rev. Ken Fleck

Dump Cake

1 can (20 oz.) undrained, crushed pineapple
1 can (20 oz.) cherry, blueberry, or *apple filling
1 box regular cake mix (2 layer);
          *spice cake (with apple filling)
1 c. chopped nuts
2 sticks margarine in evenly sliced pats
     1 t. *cinnamon (with apple filling)

In a 9x13-inch ungreased pan, spread crushed pineapple and pie filling. Lightly combine cake mix, nuts and margarine, then sprinkle on top. Bake at 350 degrees for 50 to 60 minutes. Serve topped with whipped cream or ice cream, if desired.

These ingredients complement each other.

Rev. Terrence A. McCarthy

Easier Still Dessert

Take your favorite pound cake. Slice fresh fruit and top with Cool Whip.

Take the same pound cake and slice it into fingers of cake. Arrange on a dessert plate in a star pattern with 6 of the fingers of cake. (You can also use sponge cake or lady fingers.) Arrange fruit in a decorative pattern even alternating kinds of fruit, e.g. strawberries and banana slices, or kiwi and strawberries, or peach crescents and pear slices. Place a dollop of whipped topping with a piece of the same fruit on top.

Rev. Ken Fleck

Easter Pie

Crust
8 c. flour
2 t. salt
2 T. baking powder
2 c. warm milk
6 eggs
1/2 c. oil

Sift flour, salt, and baking powder together and make into mound with a well in the center. Into the well add the milk, eggs, and oil. Blend into a dough and divide into 4 sections. Use 2 sections to cover the bottom of two 11x15-inch cake pans.

Filling
5 lbs. ricotta cheese
5 lbs. Italian sausage, cooked 20 minutes,
                    drained, and sliced
9 eggs
1 c. grated cheese
salt and pepper

Mix together and pour half on top of each bottom crust. Slice 7 or 8 hard cooked eggs over filling. Cover with remaining two sections of dough. Cut vents in top crust. Bake at 350 degrees for 40 minutes or until knife comes out clean. Serves 30.

Rev. Jerry Williams, O. Carm.

Fr. George's Mom's and Aunt Flo's Cranberry Ice

2 pkg. (12 oz. each) cranberries
1 pkg. (12 oz.) marshmallows
2 c. sugar
1/4 c. lemon juice
1 qt. water
2 egg whites *or* 1 c. whipped topping

Boil down water with cranberries until the cranberries split open. Periodically mash with a fork. Add sugar and bring to a boil. Add marshmallows, a little at a time, until dissolved. Add lemon juice. *Put in freezer until congealing begins. Take out, fold over, and return to freezer. Repeat 2 or 3 times. Fold in 2 egg whites, beaten to form stiff peaks (or cup of Cool Whip). Pass it through a sieve or leave as is for a more chunky consistency. Put back in freezer again. When result resembles sherbet, you are ready to enjoy! May need to fold over again.

The last directions are very important, because the last time I made the recipe the result was more a mush than ice or sherbet. Goes well with a meal or as a dessert (especially turkey).

Rev. George Morgan, CMF

Fannie May Fudge

1 stick butter *or* margarine
2 pkgs. chocolate pudding mix
1/2 c. milk
2 c. powdered sugar
2 c. walnut pieces
2 t. vanilla

Mix together and bring to a boil and continue boiling for one minute. Remove from heat and sift in powdered sugar. Add walnuts and vanilla. Pour into buttered 8-inch pan and let cool. Do not refrigerate. Cut into small squares.

Rev. Jerry Williams, O. Carm.

Frank's Fruit Slices

Pastry
4 c. flour
1 t. salt
2 sticks butter
1 c. shortening
2 eggs
4 T. cold water

Sift flour and salt. Cut in shortening with two forks or pastry cutter until pea-sized. Beat eggs with water and add to flour mixture. Mix with hands until smooth. Divide dough in half. Roll out one portion so that it will fit a cookie sheet with sides (16x11x3/4-inch jellyroll pan). Place dough in pan and up the sides.

Filling
3 cans (16 oz. each) your favorite pie filling (cherry,
peach, blueberry, apricot, apple, etc.)
(Fresh fruit can also be used. Prepare it as for a pie.)

After filling is placed in pastry shell in pan, roll out the other half of dough and place it on top as a single sheet. Pierce with a fork to let steam out. Or roll out and cut it into 1-inch strips to form a latticework. Seal each strip at the edges. Bake in a preheated oven at 400 degrees for 15 minutes. Reduce temperature to 325 degrees and continue baking for 20 minutes.

Rev. Ken Fleck

Kolaches

1 lb. butter
1 pint vanilla ice cream, softened
4 c. flour

Mix all well and form into small balls. Make an indentation with your thumb. Fill with jelly, jam, preserves, nut filling, whatever you wish. Bake for 20 minutes at 350 degrees on an ungreased sheet. Dust with powdered sugar.

Rev. Jerry Williams, O. Carm.

German Chocolate Cake

2 c. flour
1 t. baking soda
1/2 t. salt
1 4-oz. pkg. sweet baking chocolate
1 stick butter
1 1/2 c. sugar
3 eggs
1 t. vanilla extract
1 c. buttermilk

Grease and lightly flour two 8 x 2 or 9 x 2-inch round baking pans. (This can also be made in a single layer 13 x 9 x 2-inch pan. It helps to line the pans with parchment paper for easier removal.

Sift together flour, baking soda and salt. In a saucepan combine the chocolate and 1/2 c. boiling water and stir until melted. Allow to cool.

In a mixer cream the butter and sugar until fluffy, about 7 minutes. Add vanilla and eggs one at a time. On low speed add the chocolate mixture. Gradually, by alternating, add the flour mixture and the buttermilk until combined. Pour batter into prepared pans.

Bake in a pre-heated oven 350 degrees for 30 to 40 minutes. Test with a wooden toothpick inserted in the center of the cake. If it comes out clean, the cake is ready. Cool on wire cake racks for 10 minutes. To remove cakes from pans, run a thin knife around the edge of the pan to loosen. Place the wire rack on top of the pan and flip over. Gently lift the pan and remove the parchment paper. If using the larger single pan let cool completely before frosting. Use the frosting recipe which follows on the next page.

Most Rev. Raymond Goedert
Auxiliary Bishop of the Archdiocese of Chicago
Submitted by a friend as one of his favorite cakes.

German Chocolate Cake Frosting

1 egg
1 c. evaporated milk
1 c. sugar
1/2 stick (1/4 c.) butter
1-1/2 c. flaked coconut
1 c. chopped pecans

In a medium saucepan combine one beaten egg, the evaporated milk, sugar and butter. Cook over medium heat. Stir to avoid burning until thick and bubbly. Remove from heat. Stir in coconut and pecans. Allow cake to cool completely before frosting.

Most Rev. Raymond Goedert
Auxiliary Bishop of the Archdiocese of Chicago
Submitted by a friend as one of his favorite cakes.

Glazes For Cakes And Pastries

BASIC RECIPE

1 c. confectioner's sugar
2 T. butter or margarine (optional)

VANILLA

To the basic recipe add 2 t. vanilla extract and 1 to 2 T. milk as needed for consistency desired. Less for a frosting, more liquids for a drizzle.

CHOCOLATE

To the vanilla recipe add 2 to 3 T. powdered cocoa

CHOCOLATE MINT

To the basic recipe add 2 t. mint extract and 2 to 3 T. powdered cocoa.

ORANGE

To the basic recipe use orange juice instead of milk and add 1 T. orange rind or 1 T. orange juice concentrate. Strips of orange rind may be added as a garnish.

LEMON

To the basic recipe use lemon juice to taste. Start with 1 T. lemon juice and garnish with the rind of a fresh lemon thinly peeled or grated.

Rev. Ken Fleck

Gaethea's Heirloom Fig Cookies

5-1/2 sticks butter
2-1/2 c. sugar
10 eggs
3 T. vanilla extract
3 t. almond extract
1-1/2 c. milk
5 lbs. flour
6 t. baking powder

Cream butter and sugar in a mixer. Separate out 4 egg whites from the eggs and set aside. Place remaining eggs and yolks in mixer with creamed mixture. Add vanilla and almond extracts and milk. When blended transfer to a large bowl to mix in flour. Sift baking powder with first addition of flour. Gradually add the remaining flour until you have a stiff dough.

Filling

5 lbs. dried figs, ground into a paste
3 t. cinnamon
2 t. nutmeg
1 c. sugar
4 oranges, juice and zest
1 c. almonds, finely chopped

Mix all ingredients in a bowl to make filling.

With a rolling pin roll 1/4 of the dough into an oblong sheet 1/8 inch thick. Cut dough into small rectangles, about 2x4 inches, place a small finger amount of filling in the dough and fold dough over filling. Pinch ends. Place on cookie sheets in a crescent shape. Score the top 3 or 4 times.

Bake at 350 degrees for 14 to 16 minutes.

Rev. Ken Fleck

Grandma's Chocolate Cream Pie

9-inch pie shell, baked and cooled
1 pint whipping cream

Filling
1/2 c. sugar
2 T. flour
2 T. cornstarch
2 c. whole milk
2 squares unsweetened baking chocolate, coarsely grated
2 large eggs, slightly beaten
1 t. vanilla extract
1 T. butter

Sift together sugar, flour, and cornstarch. In a double boiler over medium-high heat, warm milk, then add grated chocolate and stir until chocolate melts and dissolves. Take a little of the hot milk and chocolate, and add it to the sifted dry ingredients in a separate bowl. Mix until smooth, then add this to the rest of the mixture in the double boiler. Slowly add beaten eggs, stirring the hot mixture constantly. Continue to cook filling until quite thick, about 20 minutes, stirring constantly.

Remove top pan of double boiler, and allow filling to cool for about 5 minutes. Stir in vanilla and butter. Refrigerate filling until thoroughly chilled, preferably overnight. Turn chilled filling into pie crust. In chilled bowl, whip cream until stiff. Top pie with whipped cream and serve.

Rev. Daniel A. Flens

Carol's Cool Coconut Pie

1-1/2 c. sugar
2 T. flour
1/2 stick butter *or* **margarine**
3 eggs, beaten
1 t. vanilla extract
1/2 c. buttermilk
1 c. shredded coconut

Mix all ingredients together well. Pour into an unbaked 9" pie shell. Bake at 325 degrees for 45 to 50 minutes.

Rev. Ken Fleck

Kremowke

Karol Wojtyla as a child   **Pope John Paul II**

When Pope John Paul II last visited Wadowice, Poland, he stopped at the school he attended as a child. Like a grandfather telling stories he shared his memories, one of which was his fondness for Kremowke from a local bakery. This dessert closely resembles what we commonly refer to as a "Napoleon". I have created a simpler version of this delicious dessert.

1 pkg. frozen Puff Pastry
      Use one sheet of puff pastry
2 pkg. (3.4 oz. each) vanilla pudding and pie filling
1 c. heavy cream (whipping cream)
1/2 c. semi-sweet chocolate chips
powdered sugar

Thaw the pastry sheet at room temperature, approx. 30 minutes. Preheat oven to 400 degrees. Unfold pastry on lightly floured surface. Cut into 3 strips along fold marks. Cut each strip into 3 rectangles. Place 2 inches apart on a baking sheet. Bake according to package directions, approx. 15 minutes or until golden brown. Remove from baking sheet and cool on wire rack.

Prepare the pudding according to package directions. Allow to set.

In a chilled bowl with a chilled wire beater beat the cream in a mixer until stiff peaks form.

Continued on next page.

Kremowke (cont'd)

Split the pastries into 2 layers. Spread the bottom halves with the pudding mixture. Place a generous dollop of whipped cream on top of the pudding layer. Top with remaining halves. Serve immediately with a generous dusting of powdered sugar.

Garnish with a chocolate drizzle. Simply place the chocolate chips in a plastic sandwich bag. Place the bag in a bowl of hot water for 2 minutes. Knead the bag to blend the melted chips. Snip the corner of the bag to form a piping bag.

Options: Any pudding and pie filling can be used. (I happen to like pistachio.) A substitute for the whipping cream would be 2 cups of any of the varieties of non-dairy whipped toppings. These also are flavored and can compliment the pudding you choose.

Rev. Ken Fleck

Grasshopper Pie

1-1/2 c. chocolate wafer crumbs
1/4 c. butter *or* **margarine, melted**
3 c. miniature (or **32 large) marshmallows**
1/2 c. milk
1/4 c. crème de menthe
3 T. white crème de cacao
1-1/2 c. whipping cream, whipped
few drops green food coloring (optional)

Mix wafer crumbs and butter thoroughly. Press into the bottom of a 9-inch pie pan evenly and bake in a preheated oven at 350 degrees for 10 minutes. Cool.

Combine marshmallows and milk in a saucepan. Cook over low heat stirring constantly until marshmallows melt. Cool thoroughly and add liquors. Fold marshmallow mixture into whipped cream. Fold in food coloring. Pour into crumb lined pan. Sprinkle with grated or shaved semisweet chocolate. Chill 4 hours before serving.

Rev. Ken Fleck

Kaiserschmarren

It was reported to me by my relatives in Austria that this was a favorite dessert of Pope Benedict XVI. This was also a staple of my home as a child on Fridays when we abstained from meat.

Pope Benedict XVI

6 eggs separated
1 c. pastry flour or regular flour
3 T. sugar
1 c. milk
1/2 t. vanilla extract
1/2 t. salt
1/2 c. raisins
butter and vegetable oil
powdered sugar

Separate the egg whites from the egg yolks. In a large bowl mix together the yolks, flour, sugar, milk, and vanilla. Set aside.

Beat the egg whites with a wire whisk until stiff peaks are formed. Add the salt to the egg whites after the first minute of beating. You can do this by hand or with a mixer. Gently fold the egg whites into the batter in the large bowl. Heat a large non-stick 10-inch skillet over medium heat. Add a teaspoon of oil and one pat of butter. Pour in half of the mixture and add half of the raisins sprinkled over the mixture. Cover the pan and allow to cook on one side for 2-3 minutes. Turn over or flip what is now a fluffy pancake to cook the other side for one minute. Tear or cut into pieces. Place in a warm 250 degree oven on an oven-safe serving dish. Keep warm in the oven as you prepare the second half. (The whole batch of batter can be cooked in a 12-inch skillet.)

Continued on next page.

Kaiserschmarren (cont'd)

Garnish with a generous sprinkling of powdered sugar. To compliment this dessert you may also garnish with any of the following: plum puree, whipped cream, small scoop of ice cream, fruit in season, a favorite whole fruit jam, or a fruit puree. A complimentary berry or maple syrup can be offered on the side. Serves 4.

WAFFLE OPTION

This batter can also be used to make the lightest waffles you have ever tasted. Bake in a non-stick waffle iron. Spray with a light coating of vegetable oil. Most waffle irons take 4-5 minutes for perfect waffles. The options are only limited by your imagination.

Rev. Ken Fleck

French Bread Pudding

3 eggs, slightly beaten
4 c. milk
2 t. vanilla
1 t. ground cinnamon
1/2 t. salt
3 to 4 c. day old French bread, 1-inch cubes
3/4 c. brown sugar
1/2 c. raisins (or more)

Combine eggs, milk, vanilla, cinnamon, and salt; stir in bread cubes. Stir in brown sugar and raisins. Pour mixture into 3 quart casserole round ovenware dish. Place dish in larger shallow pan on oven rack. Pour hot water into pan about 1 inch deep. Bake at 350 degrees for 45 to 60 minutes or until knife inserted halfway between center and edge comes out clean. Makes 8 servings.

Rev. John M. Murphy

New Chip on the Block

This recipe was handed onto me by my mother. I consider this my signature recipe. It produces a crisp, light, chocolate chip cookie unlike any other.

1 **stick butter**
1 **c. vegetable shortening**
2 **c. white sugar**
2 **large eggs**
1 **T. vanilla extract**
3 **c. flour**
1 **t. salt**
1 **t. baking soda**
12 oz. chocolate chips

Preheat oven 325 degrees. Set baking racks in the oven one in lower third the second in the upper third.

In a mixer cream butter, shortening and sugar until well blended on medium high. It will turn almost white. Add the eggs individually. Continue creaming. Add the vanilla. Set aside.

Sift dry ingredients twice. Add to creamed mixture folding in with a large spoon just until moistened. Add chocolate chips. Drop onto ungreased cookie sheets. (I usually use teaspoons for plain chocolate chip cookies, Tablespoons for the ones with nuts.)

Bake at 325 degrees for 16 minutes thin cookie sheets; 20 minutes on insulated cookie sheets. Rotate the cookie sheets halfway through the baking time, top to bottom. Cookies baked slow like this should not turn brown. Remove from oven. Let cool on cookie sheets for a few minutes before removing to cooling racks.

Options

Add 2 c. your favorite nut.

My favorite combinations are:

- 2 c. semi-sweet chocolate chips and 2 c. walnuts coarsely chopped
- 2 c. milk chocolate chips and 2 c. pecans coarsely chopped
- Substitute almond extract or Southern Comfort for the vanilla extract and use just 3 c. chopped pecans

Rev. Ken Fleck

Jean Stone's Cheesecake

Crust
1/4 c. margarine, melted
1-1/2 c. graham cracker crumbs
2 T. sugar

Mix margarine with graham cracker crumbs and sugar. Press into bottom of a buttered 9-inch spring form pan.

Filling
3 8oz. pkgs. cream cheese
1 c. sugar
4 eggs
1 t. vanilla

Cream the three packages of cream cheese with the sugar till fluffy. Beat in the eggs for 5 minutes. Add the vanilla. Pour into crust and place spring form pan into a larger pan with 1 inch of water surrounding the pan and bake for 50 minutes at 350 degrees. Cool in the pan. Top with sweetened sour cream, cherries, blueberries, or raspberries.

Rev. Jerry Williams, O. Carm.

Oatmeal Crispies

1/4 c. butter or Imperial margarine
1/2 c. margarine
1/2 c. granulated sugar
1 c. all-purpose flour
1-1/2 c. quick-cooking rolled oats
powdered sugar

Beat butter and margarine until creamy. Add granulated sugar and cream with margarine. Add flour and rolled oats, mix well. Chill until you can shape dough into tiny balls (about 1/2 t. per ball). Place on a cookie sheet about 2 inches apart. Flatten each ball with the bottom of a glass dipped in flour. Bake in a 350 degree oven for 12 to 15 minutes or until light brown. Remove from baking sheet and cool. Sprinkle with powdered sugar when ready to serve. Makes about 6 dozen cookies.

Rev. John J. Grace

Holiday Butter Cookies

1 c. butter (2 sticks)
1 c. sugar
1 egg
2 t. vanilla
2-1/2 c. flour
1/2 t. salt

With a mixer cream butter and sugar. Add the egg and vanilla. Sift the salt and flour. With a spoon blend into creamed mixture. Place dough in a cookie press with different plates to make holiday shapes. Dough can also be separated and a few drops of red or green food coloring may be added to each portion to make colored wreaths, trees, etc.

Some suggestions using a cookie press are:

Star Cookie: Cut a small portion of a candied cherry, red or green placed in the center, or sprinkled with multi-colored nonpariels.

Ribbon place: Make a circle (like a wreath) Decorate with two small slices of green candied cherry and one part of a red candied cherry between the two.

Be creative.

Bake at 375 degrees on an ungreased cookie sheet for 7 to 9 minutes until lightly browned. Allow to cool a few minutes before removing to a cooling rack.

Rev. Ken Fleck

Potato Chip Cookies

1/2 c. sugar
2 sticks butter
1-3/4 c. sifted flour
1/2 c. crushed potato chips
1/2 c. chopped nuts
1 t. vanilla

Mix all ingredients well. Using a teaspoon drop 2 inches apart onto ungreased cookie sheet. Bake for 12 to 15 minutes at 350 degrees. Sprinkle with powdered sugar.

Rev. Jerry Williams, O. Carm.

Lemon Squares

Crust
2 c. sifted flour
1/2 c. powdered sugar
1 c. butter

Mix together, press on bottom of cookie sheet. Bake at 350 degrees for 15 minutes.

Filling
4 eggs
2 c. sugar
1/2 c. lemon juice
1/4 c. flour
1 t. baking powder
grated rind of 1 lemon

In a bowl, beat eggs until light, gradually adding sugar and lemon juice. Sift flour with baking powder and add to batter with the lemon rind. This will have a liquid consistency. Pour into hot crust and return to oven. Bake for 25 minutes at 350 degrees Cool completely and sprinkle with powdered sugar. Cut into squares.

Rev. Jerry Williams, O. Carm.

Plenary Indulgence Pie

1 9-inch Oreo chocolate pie crust
5 large egg yolks
1 can (14 oz.) sweetened condensed milk
2/3 c. seedless raspberry jam
whipped cream
fresh raspberries for garnish

Brush one egg yolk over pie crust and bake at 350 degrees for 5 minutes. Remove and let cool. This will make the crust crunchy!

Melt jam over low heat until it has a smooth consistency. Beat 4 egg yolks, condensed milk, and melted jam until evenly blended. Pour into pie shell and bake at 350 degrees for 15 minutes. Remove and cool completely. Refrigerate at least 2 hrs. Garnish with fresh raspberries and whipped cream before serving.

Rev. Mike Zaniolo

Light 'n' Easy Cheesecake

Crust
1 c. plus 2 T. margarine, softened
2 c. flour
2 T. sugar
1 t. cinnamon
1/2 t. nutmeg (optional)

Mix together and press into a 9x13x2 inch cake pan. Bake at 350 degrees for 20 to 25 minutes. Allow to cool completely before filling.

Filling
2 large pkgs. (16 oz. each) cream cheese, softened
2 c. powdered sugar
2 t. vanilla
2 pkgs. Dream Whip, follow package directions
       (*or* 4 c. Cool Whip)

Let cream cheese soften (about 40 seconds in a microwave at medium). Cream with a mixer gradually adding powdered sugar and vanilla. Fold in Cool Whip. Pour into cooled crust. Refrigerate for 2 hours or longer.

Before serving spread a can of blueberry or cherry pie filling on top. Can be prepared ahead of time for an elegant, light dessert.

Rev. Ken Fleck

Pumpkin or Sweet Potato Pie

2 c. mashed pumpkin after it is cooked and well drained *or* mashed
    sweet potato
2 c. sugar
4 eggs
1 can (about 10 oz.) Pet evaporated milk
1 stick margarine, melted
6 T. flour
1 t. Pumpkin Pie Spice
2 T. vanilla extract
1 T. lemon juice (optional)
3 8-inch unbaked pie crusts

Place sugar, eggs, milk, flour, spice, vanilla, and lemon juice into a mixer and mix well. Pour into 3 8-inch pie crusts. Bake 350 degrees for 55 to 60 minutes, or until knife inserted in center comes out clean.

Rev. Ken Fleck

Lizzie's Hermits

1/2 c. vegetable shortening
1-1/2 c. brown sugar
2 eggs
3 T. milk
2-1/4 c. flour
1/2 t. allspice
1 t. baking soda
1/2 t. cinnamon
1 c. currants
1 c. chopped pitted dates
1 c. raisins
1/2 c. chopped walnuts or pecans

With a mixer, cream shortening with brown sugar. Add eggs and milk. Mix until well blended. Sift together flour, allspice, baking soda, and cinnamon.

Add dry ingredients to creamed mixture. Stir in currants, dates, raisins, and nuts. Drop by teaspoonfuls onto an ungreased cookie sheet. Bake at 325 degrees for 12 to 14 minutes. Allow to cool for a few minutes before removing to a cooling rack.

Rev. Ken Fleck

Oreo Cookie Cake

1 pkg. Oreo cookies
1 stick margarine, melted
1/2 gallon vanilla ice cream
1 jar caramel or fudge topping
1 ctn. (12 oz.) Cool Whip

Chop cookies in blender or food processor. Reserve 1/2 cup. Mix remaining with margarine. Spray a 9x13 inch pan with nonstick vegetable spray. Spread cookie mixture evenly in bottom and pat down. Slice ice cream into 1/2 inch slices and place on crust. Put topping over ice cream. Spread Cool Whip on top of that and sprinkle with reserved cookies. Freeze. Serves 12. Enjoy!!

Rev. Richard Ehrens

Mary's Chocolate Cookies

5-1/2 sticks butter
2-1/2 c. sugar
10 eggs
4 T. cocoa powder
3 t. cinnamon
3 t. allspice
1 1/2 c. milk
6 t. baking powder
5 lbs. flour

Cream butter and sugar in a mixer. Separate out 4 egg whites from the eggs and set aside. Place remaining eggs and yolks in mixer with creamed mixture. Add cocoa, cinnamon, and allspice, and milk. When blended transfer to a large bowl to mix in flour. Sift baking powder with first addition of flour. Gradually add the remaining flour until you have a stiff dough.

Roll dough into 3/4-inch diameter ropes. In creative ways place dough on cookie sheets, e.g. braided, pretzel knots, canes, bows, etc. Bake at 350 degrees for 14 to 16 minutes.

Icing
4 egg whites you reserved
3 t. vanilla extract
3 t. almond extract
1-1/2 c. powdered sugar

Beat egg whites, vanilla, and almond extracts in a small bowl with a fork. Gradually add the powdered sugar until blended and smooth. Glaze cookies lightly.

Rev. Ken Fleck

Meringue

Can be used on a variety of pies from lemon to pumpkin, sweet potato, baked Alaska, etc.

3 egg whites
pinch of salt (about 1/8 t.)
1/4 t. cream of tartar
6 T. sugar
1 t. vanilla extract

With a mixer beat egg whites, salt and cream of tartar until they begin to stiffen. Beat in sugar gradually, 1 T. at a time. Add vanilla. Continue beating until meringue forms stiff peaks. Spread on pie or cake. Brown in oven set at 400 degrees for 5 to 8 minutes.

On Baked Alaska meringue is spread on a core of frozen cake and ice cream and can be stored in the freezer until dessert time when it is placed in the oven.

Rev. Ken Fleck

No Yeast Kolaczki

2 sticks butter or margarine
1/2 c. sugar
1 t. vanilla
2 egg yolks
2 c. flour
1/2 t. salt
assorted pastry toppings

Cream butter; add sugar and vanilla. Beat egg yolks together and add to the creamed butter and sugar. Mix flour and salt; add to creamed mixture. Roll out the dough. Cut into 2" circles and top with desired fruit fillings. (My favorite is powidła) Bake at 375 degrees for 15 minutes or until done. Sprinkle powdered sugar on top when cool. Make one batch at a time and start the diet next week!

Rev. Stanley G. Rataj

Nut Cake

1/2 lb. butter
2 c. sugar
3 c. self-rising flour
    (or add 2 T. baking powder and 1 t. baking soda
          to 3 cups sifted all purpose flour)
6 eggs
2 t. vanilla
1 lb. walnuts, finely chopped

Cream butter and sugar until fluffy. Gradually add flour, mix until blended. Beat in eggs, one at a time. Add vanilla and fold in walnuts. Pour into greased and lightly floured tube pan.

Bake at 350 degrees for 1-1/2 hours.

> BOOZER'S NOTE: For extra rich holiday flavor, prick warm nut cake with toothpicks and pour 1/2 c. bourbon over the top of the cake. Allow to mellow for at least one day.

Rev. Edwin Bohula (Capt., CHC, USN, Ret.)

Orange Topped Angel

1 pkg. white angel food cake mix
2 t. grated orange peel

Frosting:
1/3 c. butter or margarine softened
3 c. powdered sugar
2 t. grated orange peel
2 T. orange juice

Prepare cake mix according to box directions. After beating, fold in 2 t. orange peel. Pour into angel food pan and bake as the box instructs.

For Frosting, blend butter and sugar at low speed. Stir in orange peel and juice. Beat at medium speed until smooth. If necessary, stir in additional orange juice, 1/2 t. at a time until desired consistency is reached. Frost cake. Garnish with orange zest, if desired.

Rev. Edwin Bohula (Capt., CHC, USN, Ret.)

Peach Kuchen

1 box white cake mix
1/2 c. flaked coconut
1/2 c. butter or margarine

<u>Peach Topping:</u>
1 can (1 lb.13 oz.) peaches, drained
2 T. sugar
1/2 t. cinnamon
1 c. sour cream
1 egg slightly beaten

Preheat oven to 350 degrees.

Combine cake mix and coconut. Cut in butter until coarse-like crumbs are formed. Press <u>lightly</u> onto bottom and sides of a 9x13 inch pan. Bake at 350 degrees for 10 to 15 minutes.

Arrange peach slices on baked mixture and sprinkle with sugar/cinnamon mixture. Combine sour cream and beaten egg and pour over all. Return to oven and bake 10 minutes, just until sour cream is set.

Serves 10 to 12.

Rev. Edwin Bohula (Capt., CHC, USN, Ret.)

Pear Ice

1 c. sugar
2 ripe medium pears, peeled and cored
1 T. lemon juice
pear liqueur
pear slices brushed with lemon juice, for garnish

In a small saucepan combine sugar with 1 c. water. Cook over high heat, stirring, until sugar dissolves. Pour the syrup into a bowl to cool.

In a blender, combine pears and lemon juice. Puree and with the machine running, add pear liqueur. Pour into an ice cream maker and freeze till the pear ice is firm. Garnish.

Rev. Jerry Williams, O. Carm.

Pie Crust

1-1/4 c. vegetable shortening
1 t. salt
3 c. flour
1 egg
1 T. white vinegar
5 T. ice water

Mix the shortening, salt, and flour with two forks or a pastry cutter until it forms beads the size of little peas. (If using a food processor, pulse until the size of peas.)

Beat the egg, vinegar, and water together:

Gradually add to the dough mixture until well blended. Dough should be soft and pliable. Divide in half. Wrap in plastic wrap and refrigerate for 30 minutes. Chilled dough is easier to handle.

Flour pastry cloth or board. Flatten one dough ball on floured surface, dust lightly with flour, flour rolling pin. Roll to desired thickness to fit your pie pan. (Dough may be rolled between two plastic wrap sheets.)

Recipe makes two pie crusts or one double crust pie.

If baking the pie crust for later use, prick the dough with a fork to let out steam and prevent bubbles. Bake with a sheet of aluminum foil fitted over crust and another pie dish on top to help it hold its shape, 375 degrees 15 minutes. Let cool completely before storing. It should be used within three days or frozen for use within three months.

Rev. Ken Fleck

Uncle Gene's Cherry Delight

1 plain angel food cake
2 pkgs. (3-1/2 oz. each) vanilla or lemon instant pudding
2 cans (20 oz.) cherry pie filling
whipped cream

Shred angel food cake into bite size pieces. Prepare pudding as instructed on package. Place shredded cake on bottom of ungreased 9x13-inch covered cake pan. Pour prepared pudding over cake. Next add a layer of pie filling spreading evenly over the pudding and cake. Cover and refrigerate 4 hrs. or overnight. Slice into generous sized squares and top with a dollop of whipped cream. Substitute apple pie filling or cranberry sauce in place of cherry filling, using vanilla pudding.

Rev. Gene Burns

Popcorn Cake

2/3 c. unpopped popcorn
1 stick butter
1/2 c. vegetable oil
1 lb. pkg. small marshmallows
1 lb. dry roasted peanuts
1 lb. M&M candy

Pop popcorn. In a pan, melt butter with oil. Add marshmallows and melt.
Add the peanuts and M&Ms. Pour over popped popcorn and mix well.
Pack tightly in a buttered tube pan and refrigerate. Cut with a serrated
knife.

Rev. Jerry Williams, O. Carm.

Pumpkin Bars

2 c. flour
2 t. baking powder
1 t. baking soda
1/2 t. salt
2 t. cinnamon
1 t. pumpkin pie spice
2 c. sugar
1 c. salad oil
4 eggs
1 can (16 oz.) pumpkin
1 c. chopped walnuts

Frosting
6 oz. cream cheese
1/4 lb. butter or margarine
1 lb. powdered sugar
1 c. chopped nuts, sprinkled on top

Combine all ingredients. Pour into greased 11x17 inch pan. Bake at 350
degrees for 20 to 25 minutes or until a knife inserted in the center comes
out clean. Cool completely.

Mix cream cheese, butter, and powdered sugar until creamy. Frost and top
with chopped nuts.

Rev. Ken Fleck

Robert's Raisin Rum Cake

1 c. golden raisins
1 box (18 oz.) yellow cake mix
1 pkg. (4 oz.) vanilla instant pudding
4 eggs
1/2 c. water
1/2 c. vegetable oil
1/2 c. dark rum

Grease and flour a 10-inch tube pan or a 12-cup bundt pan. Mix all ingredients together. (A mixer can be used but is not necessary.) Pour batter into pan. Bake in a preheated oven at 325 degrees for 60 minutes. Cool completely. Invert on a serving plate.

Glaze

1 stick butter or margarine
1/4 c. water
1 c. sugar
1/2 c. dark rum

Melt butter in sauce pan. Stir in water and sugar. Bring to a boil and continue boiling for 5 minutes. Stir constantly so sugar does not burn. Remove from heat. Stir in rum.

Using a fork or a skewer prick the top of the cake so the glaze penetrates. Pour glaze over cake.

Garnish

1 c. chopped pecans or walnuts may be added to the glaze or placed in the bottom of the pan before putting in the batter.

Seedless grapes dusted with powdered sugar.

A dollop of whipped cream or Cool Whip and maraschino cherries.

Rev. Ken Fleck

Ricotta Cake

1 lb. fresh ricotta cheese
3/4 c. sugar
1 t. vanilla
3 eggs
1 Duncan Hines yellow cake mix (without pudding)

Mash cheese, sugar, vanilla, and eggs with a fork until well blended. Set aside. Prepare cake mix as directed on box. Pour cake mix into a 9x13-inch greased and floured cake pan. Pour ricotta mixture slowly over the cake batter and bake accordingly to cake mix directions. Cool in refrigerator for at least 6 hours. Ricotta mix sinks to the bottom and looks like frosting. Can be served with berries, whipped cream, etc.

Rev. Jerry Williams, O. Carm.

Sour Cream Rhubarb Coffee Cake

1/2 c. brown sugar
1/2 c. margarine
1 egg
2 c. flour
1 t. baking soda
1/2 t. salt
2 c. rhubarb (cut in 1/2-inch pieces)
1 c. sour cream

Topping
1/2 c. sugar
1/2 c. chopped nuts
1 T. margarine
1 t. cinnamon

Mix topping until crumbly and set aside.

Cream brown sugar, margarine and egg. Sift flour, baking soda and salt and add to creamed mixture alternating with sour cream and rhubarb. Put in greased and floured 9x12-inch pan and sprinkle with topping. Bake at 350 degrees for 45 to 50 minutes.

Br. Leonard M. Lawrence, OFM

Rum Cookies

Dough
1 pkg. (2 t.) dry yeast
1/2 c. warm milk
4 c. flour
2 sticks butter, softened
3 T. sugar
1 egg
2 egg yolks

Filling
24 oz. apricot jam
2 T. rum
1 lb. walnuts, finely ground
2 c. sugar

Mix yeast and warm milk (115 degrees—warm to touch, not hot) in a bowl. In another bowl, mix flour and softened butter with pastry cutter or two forks. Add sugar, egg, and egg yolks. Mix in activated yeast. Knead until dough has an elastic consistency. Divide into three equal parts and let stand 30 minutes in a warm place out of drafts.

Mix the rum into the apricot jam. Mix the walnuts and sugar. Roll one portion of dough into a 10x15-inch rectangle *(the size of your cookie pan with a 3/4" lip)*. Place dough in pan. Spread with apricot jam mixture and sprinkle evenly a layer of nut mixture. Repeat two more times, placing the second and third layers in the pan over the first.

Bake at 350 degrees for 30 minutes. Trim the sides when cool and cut into diamond shapes.

Rev. Ken Fleck

Saintly Sundaes

1 can (15 oz.) fruit cocktail
1 container Cool Whip
1 box of your favorite cookies
1 dash vodka and 1 dash Grand Marnier
  for adults who like "Super Saintly Sundaes"
large wine or sundae glasses, chilled
ice cream
maraschino cherries

Drain excess juice from fruit cocktail. Mix fruit with vodka and Grand Marnier. Let stand 10 minutes to marinate. Crush cookies and place some on bottom of each glass. Layer fruit, Cool Whip, ice cream, cookies, fruit, Cool Whip, ice cream all the way to top of glass. Top with Cool Whip and maraschino cherry. Chill several hours before serving. Have sugar wafer cookies available. Think of the saints when you eat this sundae.

Rev. Christopher L. Krymski, OSM

Strawberry Dessert

3 to 4 c. (20) pretzel rods, crushed
3/4 c. melted butter
3 T. sugar
8 oz. cream cheese
8 oz. carton Cool Whip
1 c. powdered sugar
6 oz. strawberry Jell-O
2 c. boiling water
20 oz. frozen strawberries

Crush pretzels. Stir in butter and sugar. Press into 9x13-inch pan and bake for 8 minutes at 350 degrees. Cool 15 to 20 minutes. Mix together cream cheese, Cool Whip, and powdered sugar. Spread over crust. Combine Jell-O with boiling water. Add frozen strawberries and cool. When it begins to congeal, pour over cheese mixture. Chill until firm.

Br. Leonard M. Lawrence, OFM

Sweet Potato Pie

9 medium size sweet potatoes
2 sticks of butter, softened
1/2 c. white sugar
1/2 c. packed brown sugar
3 eggs, well beaten
1/2 t. salt
1/4 t. nutmeg
1 T. vanilla
1 to 2 c. milk
3 9-inch unbaked pie crusts

Cook potatoes until tender. Cut off both ends, remove skins, and cut into 2 inches chunks. Mash potatoes with butter, sugar, salt, nutmeg, and vanilla. Beat eggs and half of the milk until creamy. Pour into potatoes. Beat until well mixed with an electric mixer. Use more milk if too thick. Fill each of the pie crusts. Bake at 350 degrees for 1 hour or until filling is set. Cool before serving.

Rev. Howard Tuite
by Mrs. Christine Radford

Mom's Brownies

2 sticks margarine
2 c. sugar
4 to 5 eggs
1-1/2 c. sifted flour
4 to 5 T. cocoa
2 t. vanilla
chopped nuts, optional

Cream butter and sugar. Add eggs. Sift flour with cocoa. Mix into egg mixture. Stir in vanilla and nuts. Bake 30 minutes at 350 degrees.

Frosting
1 stick margarine
1/4 c. cocoa
1/3 c. milk
1 box powdered sugar
1 t. vanilla

Combine margarine, cocoa, and milk in a sauce pan. Heat to boiling. Continue to boil for 1 minute. Add powdered sugar and vanilla. Stir well. Pour over warm brownies and let set.

Rev. Jerry Williams, O. Carm.

Sweetheart Crescents

4 c. flour
1/2 t. salt
1 c. butter or margarine
3 egg yolks
1/2 c. sour cream
1 t. vanilla extract
1 pkg. active dry yeast
1 can pecan filling or almond paste

Sift flour and salt together. With forks or pastry cutter cut in butter until particles are fine, like small peas and shortening is incorporated. Blend 3 egg yolks with sour cream. Add vanilla and yeast. Mix well. Add to the flour mixture and mix well to form a dough. Let it rest for 10 minutes.

Divide dough into four parts. Roll out each part on a surface sprinkled with sugar. Roll to an 11-inch circle about 1/8-inch thick. Spread with filling. With a pizza cutter divide circle into eight parts. Starting with wide end roll to the point. Place on a greased baking sheet with point side down, curving the ends to from crescents. Bake at 325 degrees for 10 to 12 minutes.

Rev. Ken Fleck

Butter Pecan Squares

2 c. graham crackers, crushed
1 lb. powdered sugar
1-1/2 sticks of margarine, melted
12 oz. bag semi-sweet morsels
18 oz. jar crunchy peanut butter

Melt margarine and pour over crushed crackers and mix well. Add peanut butter and powdered sugar. Mix well. Pack firmly into 9x12-inch pan. Roll a glass over it to make sure it's solid. Melt chocolate chips and spread on top. Refrigerate to harden. Remove from refrigerator, bring to room temperature, and cut in squares.

Rev. Thomas S. Boyle

Tomascin Honey Cake

Cake
3-1/2 c. flour
1/2 t. baking soda
1 t. baking powder
1-1/2 T. butter
6 T. milk
1-1/2 c. sugar
2 eggs
3 heaping T. honey

Sift together flour, baking soda, and baking powder. Set aside. In a double boiler cook the butter, milk, sugar, eggs, and honey for 3 to 5 minutes. Pour hot mixture into the flour and mix quickly. Divide dough into 4 parts and keep them well covered with a towel to prevent forming a crust. Dust a rolling board well with flour. Roll dough into a rectangular shape, slightly smaller than a cookie sheet.

Place rolled dough on a well-greased cookie sheet and bake at 350 degrees for 10 minutes or until a medium brown color. Repeat this for the remaining balls of dough, remembering to regrease the pan before baking each layer. Once baked, flip each layer onto a towel to cool. The sheets will turn hard-not to worry! When all are baked and cooled, fill with the following mixture.

Filling
2 c. milk
4-1/2 T. Cream of Wheat hot cereal
dash of salt
1/2 lb. butter
3/4 c. powdered sugar
1 t. vanilla

Heat milk, Cream of Wheat, and salt for 5 minutes. Set aside and cool. Cream butter, powdered sugar, and vanilla. Slowly blend in the cooled Cream of Wheat. Divide filling into 3 parts. Spread filling evenly between cake layers, finishing with a cake layer on top. Cover and refrigerate for a day or two to allow the cake to moisten. Cut into diamond shaped squares and sprinkle with powdered sugar. Delicious!

Rev. Jerry Williams, O. Carm.

Turtle Cake

1 box Pillsbury Plus chocolate cake mix
1/2 c. milk
3/4 c. margarine, soft
2/3 c. Carnation canned milk
1 (6 oz.) bag chocolate chips
1/2 c. pecan halves
1 bag caramels

Make cake mix as directed adding 1/2 c. milk and 3/4 c. margarine to batter. Pour 1/2 the batter into a prepared 13x9 inch baking dish and bake at 350 degrees for 15 minutes. While cake is baking melt caramels and 2/3 cup Carnation milk over low heat stirring constantly.

Take cake out after 15 minutes and spread chocolate chips and nuts over top of the cake, then pour the caramel mixture over all that. Pour rest of cake batter over the top. Return to oven and continue to bake for 30 to 40 minutes or until cake is done.

Let cool at least 1 hour. Frost with sour cream or cream cheese frosting.

Rev. Edwin Bohula (Capt., CHC, USN, Ret.)

Fudge Sauce

1 stick butter (DO NOT USE MARGARINE)
1 box powdered sugar
1 c. evaporated milk
1/2 lb. bitter chocolate
1/8 t. salt
1/2 c. miniature marshmallows
1 t. vanilla

Melt the above ingredients in top of double boiler. Stir occasionally. Sauce is done when marshmallows are dissolved. Add 1 t. vanilla. Cool and refrigerate.

Sauce is great for ice cream and pound cake. Makes about 2 cups of sauce.

Rev. Edwin Bohula (Capt., CHC, USN, Ret.)

Vera's Viennese Wunderbars

2 c. sifted flour
1 t. baking powder
1/2 t. salt
1/2 c. sugar
2/3 c. butter
4 egg yolks, slightly beaten
2 T. milk
1 t. lemon juice
1 c. apricot or raspberry jam
4 egg whites
1/2 c. sugar
1 c. ground walnuts

Sift flour, baking powder, salt and sugar together. Cut in butter with two forks or pastry blender until it is the size of small peas. Mix in a separate bowl egg yolks, milk, and lemon juice. Add to dry ingredients and mix well. Press in the bottom and about 1/2 inch up the sides of a 9x13-inch pan. Spread your favorite jam over this pastry base.

With a mixer beat egg whites until stiff peaks form and gradually add sugar. Take from mixer and fold in ground nuts. Place evenly on jam filling. Bake at 350 degrees for 30 minutes. Cool and cut into squares or diamonds.

Rev. Ken Fleck

Dan's Delight

1 cup lemon-flavored fat-free or low-fat yogurt
1 cup fresh blueberries or sliced strawberries
3 plain or cinnamon graham crackers

Crumble the graham crackers and place in the bottom of a cereal bowl. Place the yogurt on top of the crackers evenly. Arrange the blueberries in a pattern of choice, e.g. the letter initial of the person you are making it for, a star, concentric circles, etc.

Serves one with a cheesecake flavor but half the calories and all the satisfaction.

Rev. Ken Fleck

Walnut Torte

8 eggs separated
1 c. sugar
1-3/4 c. (8 oz.) ground walnuts
1 c. dry breadcrumbs

Beat egg yolks in mixer until thick and lemon-colored. Gradually add sugar until mixture is thick and falls from the beaters in heavy ribbons. In a separate bowl, beat egg whites until stiff but not dry. Sprinkle nuts and bread crumbs over yolks. Fold egg whites into yolk mixture. Turn the batter into a greased 10-inch tube pan. Bake in a 300 degree oven for 50 to 60 minutes or until a food pick inserted near the center comes out clean. Let cool in the pan at least 10 minutes. Turn onto a wire rack to cool completely. Frost top and sides with coffee frosting.

Coffee Frosting
3 sticks butter or margarine, softened
1 box (16 oz.) powdered sugar
4 t. dark rum, warmed
2 T. instant coffee

Gradually beat sugar into softened butter. Dissolve coffee in warm rum and add to frosting. Makes enough to frost one cake. Serves 12-15.

Cake may also be baked in a bundt pan and served without frosting but garnished with a dollop of whipped cream/topping and chocolate shavings.

Rev. Ken Fleck

Easy Coconut Cream Pie

4 eggs
1 stick butter *or* margarine, softened
3/4 c. sugar
1 c. shredded coconut
2 c. milk
1/2 c. flour

Place ingredients IN ORDER into a blender. Blend one minute. Pour into a greased 9-inch pie plate. Bake 1 hour at 350 degrees. Makes its own crust.

Rev. Jerry Williams, O. Carm.

Schnecken

Although this translates as "snails", this dessert was a mainstay in my family from childhood on. The sweet roll dough used in this recipe can be used for a variety of other recipes as well. On a cold winter morning, after delivering newspapers, nothing warmed the Fleck boys inside and out as these rolls fresh from the oven.

2 pkgs. (5 t.) dry yeast
1/2 c. warm water
1 c. warm milk
1/2 c. sugar
1 t. salt
1/2 c. vegetable shortening or butter
4-1/2 to 5 c. flour
2 eggs
syrup
cinnamon sugar
1/2 c. raisins

Caramel Sauce

Melt in a saucepan:

      1/2 c. butter
      4 T. corn syrup or maple
      1 c. brown sugar
      1 c. walnuts or pecans

Schnecken (cont'd)

Dissolve the yeast in the warm water along with a pinch of sugar to help feed the yeast.

In a mixer combine the warm milk, sugar, salt, shortening, and 2 cups of flour. Beat until smooth. Add the eggs one at a time. Add yeast mixture. Mix in remaining flour scraping the sides of the bowl until it forms a ball around the mixer dough hook and cleans the side of the bowl. It will be slightly sticky.

Place the dough onto a lightly floured clean surface. Knead until smooth and elastic. It should be soft and slightly warm to your touch. Mix in enough remaining flour so that it is easy to handle. Place in a greased bowl. Flip the dough upside down. Cover and let rise in a warm place until double (about one hour). I usually warm the oven for one minute, turn it off, then place the covered bowl of dough inside and let it rise.

Place dough on lightly floured clean surface. Cut in half. Roll into a rectangle about 12 x 18 inches and approx. 1/4 inch thick. Brush with melted butter. Sprinkle with cinnamon sugar (1 T. cinnamon to 1 c. sugar), add raisins. Roll into an 18-inch log. With a sharp knife cut 1 to 1 1/2 inch slices. In a greased 8x8 inch pan place one half of the caramel sauce. Sprinkle with coarsely chopped walnuts or pecan halves. Place the dough swirls on their sides with 1/2 inch space between the rolls. Repeat with second half of dough into a second pan.

Let rise until double, about 30 minutes The upside down swirls resemble snails, hence the name, *Schnecken*, aka "Sticky Buns" or caramel cinnamon rolls.

Bake in a pre-heated oven at 375 degrees for 25 to 30 minutes. Remove from oven. Place wire cooling rack on top of pan, flip over and allow to rest for 3-5 minutes before removing pan. This allows the caramel sauce to fix atop the sweet rolls. **Caution**: Hot caramel sauce can cause severe burns.

Rev. Ken Fleck

Poppy Seed Strudel
(Coffee Cake)

Take the recipe for the *Schnecken* sweet roll dough. Use half the dough for each coffee cake. Roll into a rectangle approximately 12x18 inches. Spread 1 can (12~13 oz.) of Solo brand or other poppy seed filling evenly over the dough keeping 1/2 inch border. Sprinkle with 1/2 c. dark raisins, roll into a log tucking the ends under the strudel roll. Place seam side down on a lightly greased cookie sheet. Two rolls may be baked on the same cookie sheet.

Allow to rise for 30 minutes. Bake in a preheated 375 degree oven for 25-30 minutes. Allow to cool for 30 minutes before removing to a wire rack.

Nut Strudel

Take the recipe for the *Schnecken* sweet roll dough. Use half the dough for each coffee cake. Roll into a 12x18 inch rectangle. Spread one can, (12-13 oz.) of Solo brand Almond or Nut Filling evenly over the dough keeping a 1/2 inch border. On top of the filling sprinkle finely chopped walnuts or pecans. Roll into a log tucking the ends under the strudel roll. Place seam side down on a lightly greased cookie sheet. Allow to rise for 30 minutes. Bake in a preheated oven 375 degrees for 25-30 minutes. Allow to cool for 30 minutes before removing to a wire rack.

Apricot Strudel

Follow the recipe formula as for the other strudels using instead one can of Apricot filling. Sprinkle with coarsely chopped dried apricots or use 1/2 c. golden raisins. Roll into a log placing seam side down on a lightly greased cookie sheet and bake as above.

As you can see there is a pattern here which encourages your creativity with different fillings and combinations which compliment each other.

When the strudel logs are completely cooled you can garnish them with powdered sugar before serving, or a simple icing of powdered sugar and 1 T. milk mixed to the consistency you desire from a thin glaze to a thick frosting.

Rev. Ken Fleck

Oatmeal Carrot Cookies

3/4 c. margarine, butter, or vegetable shortening
1-3/4 c. all-purpose flour
3/4 c. packed brown sugar
1/2 c. granulated sugar
1 egg
1 t. baking powder
1 t. vanilla
1/2 t. ground cinnamon
1/4 t. baking soda
1/4 t. ground cloves
2 c. rolled oats
1 c. finely shredded carrots
1/2 c. raisins (optional)

In a large mixing bowl, beat margarine or butter with an electric mixer on medium to high speed for 30 seconds or until softened. Add half of the flour, brown sugar, sugar, egg, baking powder, vanilla, cinnamon, baking soda, and cloves. Beat until combined, scraping the sides of the bowl occasionally. Beat or stir in remaining flour. Stir in oats, carrots and raisins, if desired. Drop dough by rounded teaspoons 2 inches apart onto an ungreased cookie sheet. Bake in a 375 degree oven for 10 to 12 minutes or until the edges are golden. Remove from the baking sheet; cool on a wire rack. Makes about 4 dozen.

Rev. Ken Fleck

Pecan Balls

2 sticks butter
1/2 c. sugar
2 t. vanilla
2 c. ground pecans
2 c. flour
powdered sugar

In a mixer, cream butter and sugar. Add vanilla, nuts, and flour. Mix with a spoon. Shape into balls the size of large marbles. Bake in a slow oven, 300 degrees for 30 to 40 minutes. Do not let them brown or they may burn. Store in an air tight container. Dust with powdered sugar before serving. Makes about 60.

Rev. Ken Fleck

Summer Peaches and Raspberries

5 large ripe peaches
2 c. fresh raspberries
1/4 c. vanilla sugar (see below)

Bring a large pot of water to a boil. Drop the peaches in one at a time and scald for 1-2 minutes. Using a slotted spoon remove the peaches to a bowl of cold water. Remove the skin and discard.. Place three of the peaches cut into smaller chunks into a food processor. Add 2 T. of vanilla sugar and puree. Spread the puree evenly on the bottom of a 10 or 11 inch diameter serving dish. Cut the remaining two peaches into 16 even slices. Place in a bowl with 1 T. of the sugar and toss lightly coating them.   Arrange peaches on the platter in a circle on top of the peach puree around the edge of the serving dish. This may be made 3 to 4 hours ahead of time and refrigerated.

When ready to serve toss the raspberries with the remaining sugar. Place in the center of the serving tray with the peaches. This may be served by itself or as a side to vanilla ice cream or a vanilla or peach custard.

Rev. Ken Fleck

Vanilla Sugar

4 plump moist vanilla beans
4 c. white sugar

Cut vanilla beans in half lengthwise.   Remove seeds for other uses. Combine the pods and sugar in a tightly covered jar for several days. May be stored indefinitely. As you use the sugar, add more to keep your supply on hand.

Rev. Ken Fleck

Ice Cream Watermelon Mirage

2 to 3 quart smooth glass or metal bowl
1/2 gal. green pistachio ice cream or lime sorbet
1/2 gal. red raspberry sorbet or strawberry ice cream
1 c. semisweet chocolate chips

Chill bowl in freezer. Allow ice creams and sorbet to soften, not melt, at room temperature, so that it is easier to mold. Press the green ice cream or sorbet to form a 1-inch thick layer on the inside of the bowl up to the rim. Mix the chocolate chips into the red sorbet or ice cream. Press into the center of the green ice cream shell filling the center. Return to the freezer until ready to serve.

When ready to serve dip bowl of ice cream into a bath of warm water for 20 seconds without letting water get into the ice cream. Place a serving plate on top and flip to remove ice cream from bowl. This can be garnished with green and red grapes that have been either frozen or dusted with powdered sugar.

Rev. Ken Fleck

Heath Bar Coffee Cake

2 c. flour
1 stick butter
1 c. brown sugar
1/2 c. white sugar
crumb-like pie crust
1 c. buttermilk
2 eggs
1 t. baking soda
4 Heath bars
1/2 c. chopped nuts

Line 9-inch pie pan with crumb crust, but set aside 1/2 c. of the mixture.

Mix flour, butter, and sugars. Add buttermilk, eggs, and baking soda. Pour into pan. Cover with chopped Heath pieces, nuts and the 1/2 c. cup of crumb crust mixture. Bake at 350 degrees for 30 minutes.

Rev. Thomas J Purtell

Chocolate Candies

1/2 lb. milk chocolate or white chocolate
     or dark chocolate
     or semi sweet chocolate chips
dry roasted peanuts
sliced almonds, walnut halves
candied cherries, red and green
multi-colored chocolate shots
pretzel rods 8 to 10 inches long
medium crisscross pretzels

CHOCOLATE BARK

1/2 c. your favorite chocolate melted in either a double boiler or in a microwave for 90 seconds on HIGH. If more time is needed give it ten seconds and stir. DO NOT OVERCOOK. If the chocolate is too thick, thin only with 1-2 teaspoons shortening. Mix in 1 cup of your favorite nuts. Spread mixture on a waxed paper-lined cookie sheet or pan. Let cool. Quicker cooling in the refrigerator or freezer. Break into small serving sizes. Store in a cool dry place with waxed paper between layers.

BIRCH BARK

Use white chocolate for recipe above.

CALIFORNIA BIRCH BARK

Use whole roasted almonds in first recipe.

PEPPERMINT PATTIES

Take your old peppermint Christmas canes, pulverize them in a blender or smash them in a plastic baggie with a hammer or meat tenderizer or a small skillet. Blend 1 cup of peppermint chips into white chocolate.

HOT RODS

Pretzel rods dipped half way into white chocolate. Sprinkle with red or green sugar crystals or with multi-colored chocolate shots. Dip more pretzel rods half way into dark chocolate and sprinkle with red or green sugar crystals.

PIANO PRETZELS

Take medium crisscross pretzels. Dip one half in white chocolate and let cool, dip the other half in dark or milk chocolate and cool. Store in cool dry place.

Continued on Next Page

FLYING SAUCERS

Take vanilla wafers, dip in your favorite chocolate, top white chocolate ones with half of a candied red or green cherry, top milk chocolate dipped wafers with a slivered almond or a walnut half

YOYOS

Spread your favorite peanut butter on vanilla wafers. Dip in milk chocolate and top with chopped peanuts or sprinkle with ground walnuts or ground pecans.

CANDY CUPS

Take your favorite recipe for Chocolate Bark or Birch Bark or California Bark, place about one tablespoonful in small paper cups, for white chocolate top with a red or green cherry, for milk chocolate top with either a walnut half, pecan, or slivered almonds.

PEANUT BUTTER CUPS

Pour milk chocolate about 1/4" deep into paper muffin cups, let cool for 5-10 minutes, place a tablespoon of your favorite peanut butter on top of the chocolate. Heat oven to 350 degrees and bake for 5 minutes or until peanut butter has leveled out.

Rev. Ken Fleck

Here are recipes galore
To test, to taste, to serve and then
One, two, three, four,
To glorify You, Lord! Amen.

Irene Hayes
St. George Parish

Oatmeal Cookies

1 c. (2 sticks) margarine
1 c. brown sugar
1/2 c. white sugar
2 eggs
1 t. vanilla
1 t. baking soda
1 t. cinnamon
1/2 t. salt
1-1/2 c. flour
3 c. oatmeal
1 c. raisins (optional)

Cream margarine, sugars, and eggs. Add vanilla, soda, cinnamon, and salt. Add flour and oatmeal (also raisins if desired). Drop by spoon on cookie sheet. Bake at 350 degrees for 7-10 minutes.

Rev. Bernard Kennedy, OFM

Peanut Butter Cookies

3/4 c. peanut butter
1/2 c. vegetable shortening
1-1/4 c. firmly packed light brown sugar
3 T. milk
1 T. vanilla
1 egg
1-3/4 c. flour
3/4 t. salt
3/4 t. baking soda

Preheat oven to 375 degrees. Combine peanut butter, shortening, brown sugar, milk, and vanilla in large bowl. Beat at medium speed with electric mixer until well blended. Add egg and beat just until blended. Combine flour, salt, and baking soda. Add to creamed mixture at low speed. Mix just until blended.

Drop unto ungreased cookie sheet 2 in. apart and flatten slightly in criss-cross pattern with a fork. Bake at 375 degrees for 7 to 8 minutes, or until set or just beginning to brown. Cool 2 minutes on baking sheet, then remove from sheet and cool completely on a wire rack.

Rev. Ken Fleck

Peanut Butter Blossoms

1/2 c. butter
1/3 c. peanut butter
1/2 c. white sugar
1/2 c. brown sugar
1 egg
1 t. vanilla extract
1-3/4 c. flour
1 t. baking soda
1/2 t. salt
Hershey's candy kisses

Mix the butter and peanut butter. Mix in sugars, egg, and vanilla. Then gradually add flour, baking soda, and salt. Mix well.

Shape into balls and roll in sugar. Place on a greased cookie sheet. Bake at 350 degrees for 10 – 12 minutes. Place a Hershey's kiss in the middle of each cookie and bake for 2 more minutes.

Br. Ivan Weis

Saint Aquin Chocolate Chip Cookies

2 c. flour, sifted
1 t. baking soda
1/2 t. salt
1 c. butter
1/2 c. granulated sugar
3/4 c. brown sugar
2 t. vanilla
1 egg
2 c. (12 oz.) chocolate chips

Preheat oven to 375 degrees.
Sift together the flour, baking soda, & salt. Set aside.
Cream the butter and sugars together until fluffy. Add the vanilla and egg. Mix well. Add the sifted dry ingredients to the creamed mixture, mix well. Fold in the chocolate chips.
Take a heaping T. of dough and roll into a ball. Place balls 2 inches apart on an ungreased cookie sheet. Bake at 375 degrees for 10 or 12 minutes.
Remove from cookie sheet and place cookies on a cooling rack.
Makes about 3-1/2 dozen cookies.

Br. Ivan Weis

Holiday Rum Balls

3 c. vanilla wafer crumbs
   (Crush in a freezer baggie with a rolling pin or in a blender.)
2 c. powdered sugar
1 c. ground nut meats — pecans, walnuts, ..., your favorite
   (Can be ground in a blender.)
1/3 c. light corn syrup
8 oz. chocolate chips
2/3 c. your favorite flavoring – rum, amaretto, raspberry brandy,
   brandy. (Non-alcoholic substitutes are raspberry syrup,
   orange juice, coconut juice, etc.)

Mix the vanilla wafer crumbs, powdered sugar, and nut meats in a large bowl.

In a double boiler melt chocolate chips and corn syrup. (Faster alternative: Microwave in a bowl for 1 minute on HIGH. Stir. Then 30 seconds on HIGH.) Add you favorite flavoring and mix until combined. Add to the mixed dry ingredients and blend.

Form into small marble-sized balls in your hands. Roll in sugar, colored sugar, nonpareils, chocolate shots, coconut flakes, etc. for a variety of textures, tastes, and decorations.

Store in an air-tight container in a cool place.

Rev. Ken Fleck

Soft Batch Cookies

Use your choice of box cake mix, e.g. Duncan Hines Devil's Food.

Change the amount of liquids to make a thicker cough. If the box cake recipe calls for adding:

1-1/4 c. water	add only	1/2 c. water
1/2 c. vegetable oil	add	1/2 c. vegetable oil
3 eggs	add	2-3 eggs

The thicker dough will be ready for your special touches. You can:

Add chopped pecans or walnuts.

Take the rind of an orange, remove and discard some of the white membrane. Chop the rind into small chips and pieces.

Add 1/2 c. chunky peanut butter.

Add peanut butter chips.

Crush old peppermint sticks in a blender and add the chips and pieces.

Use your imagination to make other variations.

Bake in a preheated oven at 375 degrees for about 12 minutes.

To stretch the Devil's Food chocolate dough and get more cookies make the box mix according to the box instructions and add:

1 c. flour
1/2 c. sugar
3 T. Hershey's baking cocoa

For other cake mixes here are some suggested additions:

To Lemon Cake Mix add: chopped orange peel
chopped cranberries and chopped walnuts
multi-colored sprinkles or chocolate shots

To German Chocolate Mix add: shredded coconut
chopped pecans
chocolate chips
vanilla (white chocolate) chips

Good luck with your creativity.

Rev. Ken Fleck

Coconut Cake

2 c. cake flour
2-1/2 t. baking powder
1/2 t. salt
2/3 c. butter or shortening
1 c. sugar
3 eggs
1 t. vanilla extract
1 c. moist shredded coconut, chopped
2/3 c milk

Preheat oven to 350 degrees. Grease two 8 inch cake pans.

Into a medium bowl sift together flour, baking powder, and salt.

Using a mixer cream butter. Add sugar gradually. Cream together until light and fluffy. Add eggs. Mix thoroughly. Add vanilla and coconut.

Fold in the flour mixture and milk a little at a time, stirring only enough after each addition to blend thoroughly. Do not beat. Pour equal amounts of batter into each cake pan.

Bake at 350 degrees for 30 minutes or until done. Frost when cool.

Soft Frosting

4 squares (4 oz.) unsweetened chocolate
3 T. hot water
1-1/4 c. powdered sugar, sifted
1 egg
1/4 c. butter, softened
1 t. vanilla extract

Melt chocolate in double boiler or microwave oven. Add hot water and stir until thick and smooth. Remove from heat. Blend in sugar and egg. Beat until smooth. Add butter, a little at a time, beating after each addition. Add vanilla and beat until blended.

Spread on cake. Sprinkle frosted cake with additional toasted coconut to you liking.

Most Rev. Raymond Goedert
Auxiliary Bishop of the Archdiocese of Chicago

Tiramisu

2 c. espresso (or regular coffee 2 times stronger than normal)
5 eggs, separated
10 T. sugar
1 lb. mascarpone (from an Italian food store)
50 lady finger cookies
baking cocoa

Prepare espresso.

Separate egg whites. Mix egg yolks with sugar.

Beat egg whites to a high fluff. Mix egg whites, egg yolks, and mascarpone in a large bowl. Mix well.

Dip lady fingers briefly into espresso and place them on the bottom of a 9x12x2 inch pan. Pour the cream mixture over the lady fingers. Place another layer of espresso-dipped lady fingers on top of the cream. Pour the remaining cream over the top. Keep refrigerated.

Place tray in freezer for 1 hour before serving.

Sprinkle 1 T baking cocoa over each portion when serving.

Rev. John Barkemeyer

Bicentennial Stars

1 pkg. Pillsbury Quick Dinner Crescent Rolls
1 c. powdered sugar
2 t. lemon extract
4 t. milk
1 can blueberry pie filling
red decorations, candied cherries, cinnamon dots, sugar crystals

Separate the triangles of dough. With the bowl of a tablespoon make an indentation in the wide part of each dough triangle.

Place 2 or 3 triangles on a lightly greased cookie sheet with the long point touching the edge of the sheet. Place 1 T. blueberry pie filling in the depression of those triangles. Place another triangle on top of each, pointing in the opposite direction. Press the edges of the pocket to seal in the filling.

Bake at 375 degrees for 10 to 13 minutes.

Let cool for 10 minutes, then top with glaze and decorate with various sprinkles and sugars.

Rev. Ken Fleck

Notes

Day Six

**The basics are ready, it's time for some just desserts.
It's amazing what one can do with cookie dough.**

"God said, "Let the earth produce every kind of living
creature: cattle, reptiles, and every kind of wild beast.""
Genesis 1:24

Something
Different

Brunch Puff

8 slices bacon
2 onions, sliced
12 slices white bread, quartered
1/2 lb. shredded Swiss cheese
8 eggs
4 c. milk
1-1/2 t. salt
1/4 t. pepper

Cook bacon until crisp, remove from pan. Crumble bacon. Cook onions in bacon drippings until soft. Place 6 slices of bread in bottom of a greased 9x13-inch cake pan. Place half the bacon, half the onions and half the cheese over the bread. Repeat the layering with the remaining bread, bacon, onions, and cheese. Combine milk, eggs, salt and pepper. Pour this mixture over bread layers. Bake at 350 degrees for 45 to 50 minutes until set and puffed. This serves 8. You can reduce it for 4 servings by cutting all ingredients by half and baking in an 8x8-inch pan.

Rev. Jerry Williams, O. Carm.

Cheese-Egg Soufflé

3 dozen scrambled eggs
2 cans (10-1/2 oz. each) cream of mushroom soup
4 T. cooking sherry
1 lb. bag of shredded cheddar cheese

Add everything and 1/2 of the cheese into a large casserole dish. Sprinkle remaining cheese on top and bake uncovered at 250 degrees for 1 hour.

Rev. Larry Lisowski

Eggs Benedict

This breakfast dish is attributed to Pope Benedict XIII, "who favored this dish for breakfast during the years he reigned (1724–1730)." As cited in "The Incredible Book of Vatican Facts and Papal Curiosities, *A Treasury of Trivia*" by Nino Lo Bello, Ligouri Publications, 1998

Pope Benedict XIII

2 English muffins
4 eggs
4 thick slices of ham or Canadian bacon
2 pkg. Hollandaise Sauce Mix

Mix the Hollandaise sauce according to package directions. Set aside. Split the English muffins, toast and butter.

Poach 4 eggs in a skillet half filled with boiling water to which you have added 1 t. white vinegar (helps to hold the eggs together). Cook until whites are solid and yolks are soft.

Warm the ham or Canadian bacon in the microwave oven or skillet. Do not overcook.

On warmed plates or a warmed platter arrange the English muffins. Place a slice of ham on each muffin. Top with a poached egg. Cover with Hollandaise sauce. Serve immediately. Serves 2.

Variations:

- Eggs can be fried or prepared over easy.
- Bread base may be thick cut toast, cornbread, or any favorite toast.
- Circles of pressed ham, slices of fried tomato, steamed spinach can be used in place of the ham or Canadian bacon.

Crocodile Curry

Personnel:
1 head chef
8 assistant chefs
4 extra chefs (standby)

Ingredients
3 large crocodiles
1 smoked warthog
3 Kg peppers
curry powder
1/2 ton rice
1 tree bay leaves

Beat crocs over heads with a sledge hammer

Collect tears in 33 gallon drums and use for salad dressing

Head chef tells assistants to place crocs into swimming pool. Turn on steam. Make sure crocs are quite dead or spare assistants may be needed.

Boil for ten days. Skin usually can be pulled off after seven days and can be used for purses, shoes, belts, etc. During the tenth day the teeth fall out and can be used for jewelry and necklaces.

Cut off tail and use for "Croc-tail" Soup. Surviving assistants cut crocs into curry cubes.

Add all other ingredients and allow to simmer for two more days.

Curry is ready when vultures start circling above. Serves approximately 1,250 people

P.S. Let your mother-in-law try it first.

Rev. Ken Fleck

Elephant Stew

1 medium sized elephant
20 bags of rock salt
500 lbs. peppercorns
800 bushels of potatoes
100 bushels of carrots
2,500 sprigs of parsley
1 rabbit & onions

Cut elephant into bite-sized pieces. This will take about six weeks.

Chop vegetables into cubes (another four weeks).

Place meat into jumbo-sized missionary pots. Pump in 1,342 gallons of elephant gravy and simmer for 28 days (until the moon reaches the same phase having gone through a full cycle).

Shovel in salt and pepper to taste. When meat is tender, add veggies. A front loader helps speed up this step.

Simmer slowly for another week. Garnish with parsley. Serves approx. 3,000 people.

If more guests are expected, add the rabbit. However, this is not really recommended because very few people like hare in their stew.

Rev. Ken Fleck

Great Gobs of Garlic

Ingredients
5 to 7 bulbs of garlic
4 to 5 T. virgin olive oil

With a sharp knife slice off the top of the garlic bulb exposing the garlic. Slice off the root end just enough so that it sits upright in a small, covered baking dish but remains together as a bulb. Drizzle the olive oil over the garlic bulbs. Cover. Bake in a 400 degree oven for 1 hour. Allow to cool for 5 to 10 minutes. Remove the garlic skins with a fork or press the garlic through a sieve to have the pure garlic, which will resemble a paste or spread that is very flavorful.

This can be stored in the refrigerator in a tightly covered container or jar for one month. Use to make garlic bread without salt, or in dips, spread on meat, flavor soups or stews. Roasting softens the harsh bite of raw garlic with a milder, distinctive flavor.

Rev. Ken Fleck

Barbara's Birthday Breakfast

2 lb. pork sausage, browned and drained
1 dozen eggs, beaten
4 c. milk
2 t. dry mustard
2 t. salt
8 slices bread, cubed
1 pkg. (8 oz). shredded cheddar cheese

Mix all together and put in 9x12-inch pan. Cover and refrigerate overnight. Bake uncovered in a 350 degree oven for one hour.

Rev. Edward F. Upton

Pancakes

As the name implies, they are simple cakes made in a pan. It may seem ridiculous to say this but it bears repeating so that cooks realize how easy they are to make. Like many other dishes, the variations are limited only by your imagination.

From scratch:
1 egg
1 c. milk
2 T. vegetable oil *or* melted butter
1 c. flour
1 T. sugar
1 t. baking powder
1/2 t. baking soda
1/2 t. salt

Combine all ingredients with a mixer and beat until well blended and smooth. This can be done by hand as well.

Heat pan or griddle until drops of water dance across surface. This is a medium high heat. If using a nonstick pan, oil is not needed to coat the pan. A pat of butter however does add to the flavor.

Pour batter from a large spoon or ladle into the pan. When batter begins to bubble, flip and turn pancakes over. Cook until golden brown.

Continued on next page

Continued from previous page.

Pancake Variations

Apple:

Add 1/2 T. cinnamon.

Substitute 1/2 c. applesauce for 1/2 c. milk into batter.

You can also just add 1/2 c. grated fresh apple into the batter.

Blueberry:

Add 1/2 c. fresh or frozen and rinsed blueberries to batter.

Cornmeal or Johnny Cakes:

Substitute 1/2 c. cornmeal for 1/2 c. flour.

Pecan or Walnut:

Coarsely chop 1/2 cup your favorite nut and add to batter.

Silver Dollar:

I remember this as a kid being a special treat.

Pour the batter by tablespoon amounts into the pan to form small round pancakes.

GARNISHES:

This is such a versatile dish that it can be used from breakfast to dessert.

Pancakes can be garnished with any of the following:

—dusted with cinnamon sugar (esp. the apple)

—dusted with powdered sugar

—green and red seedless grapes dusted with powdered sugar

—mint leaves

—peanut butter

sugar sprinkles of kids' favorite drink mixes (fruit punch, strawberry, grape, cherry, etc.)

—your favorite pie filling from a can and whipped cream

Rev. Ken Fleck

Pafleck's Monte Cristo Sandwich

2 slices bread of choice for each sandwich
   (Classic recipe calls for thick slices of bread)
Dijon mustard or stone ground mustard
4 slices or 8 oz. Swiss cheese or
   smoked Gouda or smoked cheddar
cooked turkey breast, thinly sliced
ham, thinly sliced
1/2 c. milk
4 large eggs
s & p to taste
1/4 t. nutmeg
4 T. butter
4 T. canola or vegetable oil

Preheat oven and a baking sheet to 350 degrees.

Make the sandwiches first. Spread mustard on one slice of each sandwich. (Cranberry sauce is optional on the other slice) Place the meats on each half as deep as you like. Top with cheese of choice. (Sliced cheese stays in place better than shredded.)

In a bowl whisk together the milk, eggs, S & P and nutmeg. Pour mixture onto a lipped plate or a pie dish.

Heat one large skillet or two 10-inch skillets over medium heat. Add 1 T. oil to each pan for each sandwich and 1 T. butter for flavor. Dip each sandwich into the egg mixture to coat the outside of each sandwich and lay in the pans. Cook until golden brown, 2-4 minutes. Transfer the sandwiches to the baking sheet taken from the preheated oven and bake until the cheese is melted, 5-6 minutes.

Dust with powdered sugar just before serving and cut corner to corner. I prefer to garnish with jellied cranberry sauce on the side.

Options include but are not limited to:

- raspberry jam or jelly on the turkey side of the sandwich for a spread
- low fat cheese
- egg substitutes for the real eggs.
- different breads, e.g. wheat, rye, multi-grain.

Serve with a fresh garden salad or a cucumber salad on the side. Serves four hearty appetites.

Rev. Ken Fleck

Sandwich Supreme

3 pieces bread
1 stick margarine, butter, or spread
peanut butter
grape jelly or your favorite jelly, jam, or preserve
cream cheese
1 slice American cheese or your favorite
graham cracker, optional

Spread margarine on 1 slice of bread, then put peanut butter over the margarine.

Spread jelly on second slice. Place it jelly side down on top of the peanut butter. Spread jelly on the top side of the second slice.

Spread cream cheese on third slice. Put it cheese side down on top of the jellied slice.

Place the cheese slice on top of the double-decker sandwich. Put in microwave oven. Heat for 1 minute or until cheese has begun to melt. Remove and let cool.

For extra crunch, insert graham cracker between peanut butter and jelly.

Rev. Gerald O'Reilly

Breakfast Pizza

1 lb. bulk pork breakfast sausage, browned and drained
1 pkg. (8) refrigerated crescent rolls
1 c. frozen hash brown potatoes, thawed
1 c. shredded cheddar or Monterey jack cheese
5 eggs
1/4 c. milk
1/2 t. salt
1/8 t. pepper
2 T. grated Parmesan cheese

Separate crescent rolls into 8 triangles. Place on bottom of ungreased 12-inch pizza pan with the points toward the center. Press over the bottom and up the sides to form a crust. Be sure to seal all perforations. Spoon sausage over bottom. Sprinkle potatoes over sausage. Top with shredded cheese. In a bowl, beat together eggs, milk and seasonings. Pour over crust and sprinkle Parmesan cheese on top. Bake at 375 degrees for 30 minutes.

Rev. Jerry Williams, O. Carm.

Triple-Cooked Hot Dogs

2 to 3 hot dogs
American cheese
2 pieces of bread *or* **2 hot dog buns**
ketchup
mustard *or* **horseradish**
pickle relish *or* **pickle**
diced onion
baked beans
lettuce
mayonnaise
tomato
peppers

Put hot dogs in a pan of water so they are submerged. Cover with a lid. Bring to a boil. Turn off heat and let hot dogs steam 2 to 3 minutes. Remove hot dogs with tongs and hold over stove-top flame until slightly charbroiled, rotating as needed.   Place hot dogs on bread and add ketchup, mustard, tomatoes, relish or pickle, onion, peppers, and baked beans. Top off with cheese slice. Heat in microwave 30 seconds or until cheese melts.   Add lettuce and mayonnaise after removing form microwave. Say grace before meal and dig in.

Rev. Gerald O'Reilly

Veggie Sandwiches

With all the concern about diet more people are choosing fresh vegetables in place of meat at some meals. There are limitless combinations of sand - wiches that can easily be made from your favorite vegetables and light dressings.

To limit the use of oil use a good nonstick pan. I prefer to use some extra virgin olive oil as it is healthy and adds flavor.

One large portabella mushroom cap, dry cleaned. I know that sounds strange, but mushrooms contain a lot of moisture. To clean, lightly brush with a vegetable brush rather than rinsing in water. You can also use the traditional puff ball mushroom that has been sliced.

Sauté the mushroom(s) in 1 T. olive oil. This will take about 5 minutes over medium heat. Remove the mushroom(s) to a plate. Using the oil left in the pan, perhaps adding a little, sauté one thinly sliced medium onion until tender and slightly browned.

Place the mushroom and onion in a toasted whole wheat English muffin and garnish with bean sprouts. Salt and pepper to taste.

For a little zing add a slice of jalapeno pepper cheese. If you like a sauce, rather than mayo use a light salad dressing.

Don't be afraid to experiment with different combinations of fresh vegetables, especially grilled ones like, eggplant, zucchini, and tomatoes.

Rev. Ken Fleck

OhMyGosh Omelets

3 large fresh eggs
2 T. ice cold water
1 T. olive oil
1 pat butter (optional)

A sample selection of ingredients to add:

chopped onion	small shrimp
chopped green pepper	shredded cheddar cheese
chopped ham	shredded mozzarella cheese
sliced mushrooms	grated Parmesan cheese
chopped tomatoes	Mrs. Dash
chopped dill pickle	salt and pepper to taste

Prepare the ingredients you want in your omelet ahead of time and have them arranged on a plate or in small bowls at the side of your stove. Beat the eggs and water with a whisk or fork until well mixed.

In a 10-inch nonn-stick skillet or cast iron skillet that has been heated over a medium high flame add the olive oil. After about 1 minute add the pat of butter and roll around to coat the pan. This gives a wonderful flavor to your omelet and helps it brown just right.

Add your egg mixture. It will start cooking quickly. With a fork draw the edges toward the center. It will look like a dish rag thrown into a pan loosely. Add your favorite ingredients with the cheese being the last. Cover the pan for 1 to 2 minutes. The cheese will start melting.

Loosen the omelet around the edges. Let it slide halfway out of the pan onto a serving platter. When it is halfway out, lift the pan to flip the other half of the omelet on top of the portion on the platter. It will look like a beautiful golden half moon with melted cheese oozing out the side. Omelets need to cook very quickly as described in the directions. If they cook too slowly they will turn dry. The more ingredients you pile onto your omelet the longer it will take to cook. Add 1 to 2 minutes to the cooking time.

Rev. Ken Fleck

Odds and Ends

It IS Rocket Science

In the days of Dr. Norman Vincent Peale and Dr. Robert Schuller, both of the school of the power of a Positive Mental Attitude, a popular phrase was, "Those who fail to plan, plan to fail." Good health doesn't happen automatically. It is planned and we willingly subscribe to it.

Too often we dismiss seemingly easy tasks with the cliché, "It's not rocket science." When we dismiss good health in such a way we are using an excuse for taking responsibility and giving direction to a healthy lifestyle. When we buy into the notion of convenience rather than taking time to learn and practice good nutrition we end up short changed—lacking common (cents) sense.

Doctors often tell patients that losing a few pounds will help you reduce the risk of heart disease, lower blood pressure, increase good cholesterol, and help you to sleep better. You also gain the benefit of more energy to do the things you want to do. They do not tell you *how* to lose the weight. It is not that they do not care; it is because a more skilled dietitian can take the time to understand your metabolism, body style, physical limitations, goals and timeline.

You would not put rocket fuel into a car anymore than you would put gasoline into a rocket engine and expect good results. Yet, everyday many give their bodies the wrong type of fuel to accomplish the goals they choose. *Those who fail to plan, plan to fail.*

What can we do to gain back the energy we know we should have? What can we do to shape our bodies to do what we want them to do? Make plans. Give our consent. Make a commitment to achieve our goals.

This leads to educating ourselves toward good nutrition. There are many avenues for this, namely, books, professional dieticians, regular medical check-ups, and a written plan. It sounds complicated and detailed, yet who of us would take a vacation trip without setting down plans for the whole time period. Our life's journey is an even longer trip and deserves better planning.

The first appetizer we all need to gorge ourselves on is humble pie. We like to think we don't need anyone's help. The truth of our humanity is that we all need someone sometime. When we are humble enough to ask for and seek help, we are on the right track. Those who truly love us will support us in achieving our goal—better health through better choices. What fuels does your body **need** versus what do you **want**. When we learn to make this critical commitment, we start to give our bodies the right fuel.

Plan to succeed!

"Mind Over Fatter"

"Diet" is a four-letter word that some fear as if it were a swear word, or at best, a word to be stricken from our vocabulary since it has brought most more grief than success. The current plethora of diet books uses a wide range of options to help the reader lose weight. Is there a common thread? Is there a kernel of truth? (Some books might avoid that last phrase as it is a concession to carbohydrates.) What is the middle ground—apart from the middle ground most of us are fighting with and trying to shake off?!? Aaarrrggghhh!!!

I propose that there exists a happy medium—and I am not talking about the size of our food orders alone. It is mind over matter. Is it really just in my head? Yes.

Diet books, diet programs, diet meals delivered to our homes, dieticians, and the advice we accumulate to help us lead healthy lives all begin with you giving consent. Unless you agree to follow a plan with your free will, when the restraints are taken away or the external discipline removed, you will return to the old habits that got you where you are now. The mind plays the most critical role in any choice for a healthy lifestyle.

With that key element in your defense against the battle of the bulge, if you are willing to stick to your goals, you are ready to make changes. You are ready to take the steps necessary to chart a new course for your health. (Notice the word "diet" never entered this life altering philosophy.)

For most, the word "diet" has negative connotations. It probably could be juxtaposed with the term "evil spirit". It seems imposed, whether by friends, spouse, or personal image of "what I wish for by a certain date for a certain reason". Once that goal is achieved the restraints are gone and old habits return. There is certain wisdom in Bible passages that help us reflect on this experience of "failed diets". (Luke 11:24-26 and Matthew 12:43-45.)

Choosing a healthy lifestyle is a positive action. Rather than looking back at what might have been it is an action to give a new direction to your life.

I do not endorse any particular programs to help lose weight. They all have merit and drawbacks. The underlying foundation of any successful program is that the person gives consent, commitment, and has a new vision. These are the internal forces that guarantee success. My personal gauge of success is not the scale but the balance that tells me whether or not I have the energy to do the things I want to do—consent for a positive goal.

What is your goal?

Rev. Ken Fleck

Conversion Chart for
Oven Temperatures and Dial Markings

	Number	Centigrade	Fahrenheit
Low	1/2 - 2	115 - 155	240 - 310
Med.	3 - 4	160 - 190	320 - 370
High	5	195 - 205	380 - 400
Hot	8 - 9	235 - 250	450 - 480

Dirty Dishes

Thank God for dirty dishes,
They have a tale to tell;
While others may go hungry,
We're eating very well
With home and health and happiness,
I shouldn't want to fuss;
For by the stack of evidence,
God's been very good to us.

Life's Recipes

1 c. good thoughts
1 c. kind deeds
1 c. consideration for others
2 c. sacrifice for others
3 c. forgiveness
2 c. well-beaten faults

Mix thoroughly. Add tears of joy and sorrow and sympathy for others. Fold in 4 c. of prayer and faith to lighten the other ingredients and raise texture to great heights of Christian living. After pouring all this into your daily life, bake well with warmth of human kindness. Serve with a smile.

My Kitchen Prayer

Bless my pretty kitchen, Lord,
And light it with Thy love.
Help me plan and cook my meals
From Thy heavenly home above.
Bless our meals with Thy Presence
And warm them with Thy grace;
Watch over me as I do my work
Washing pots and pans and plates.
The service I am trying to do
Is to make my family content,
So bless my eager efforts, Lord,
And make them heaven sent.

Each time you turn the pages
Looking for something new to cook
Fondly remember each person
Who makes possible this book.

Rev. Leon R. Wagner

Obituary of the Pillsbury Doughboy

Please join me in remembering a great icon. Veteran Pillsbury spokesperson, The Pillsbury Doughboy, died yesterday of a severe yeast infection and complications from repeated pokes to the belly. He was 71. Doughboy was buried in a slightly greased coffin. Dozens of celebrities turned out, including Mrs. Butterworth, the California Raisins, Hungry Jack, Betty Crocke r, the Hostess Twinkies, Captain Crunch and many others.

The graveside was piled high with flours as long-time friend, Aunt Jemima, delivered the eulogy, describing Doughboy as a man who "never knew how much he was kneaded."

Doughboy rose quickly in show business, but his later life was filled with many turnovers. He was not considered a very smart cookie, wasting much of his dough on half-baked schemes. Despite being a little flaky at times, even as a crusty old man, he was still considered a roll model for millions.

Toward the end it was thought he'd raise once again, but he was no tart.

Doughboy is survived by his second wife, Play Dough. They have two children and one in the oven. The funeral was held at 3:50 for about 20 minutes.

Day Seven

"Since on the seventh day God was finished with the work he had been doing, he rested on the seventh day from all the work he had undertaken."

Genesis 2:2

Kudos

Over eighty priests and bishops have contributed to this edition of "Burnt Offerings". I am grateful for their contributions of recipes and stories. There was a temptation to include many of the stories. The book would have been much longer.

I decided not to include their stories so that you could get to know your priests better. Ask them for their stories. Often priests strive for "transparency" in their homilies. These are times when you can get to know them through their experiences of life and faith combined. It is in the telling and sharing of stories that we grow closer to each other, especially as we understand one another better. It takes time.

In my "Dedication" I mentioned how important time is.

Preparing and serving food not only handles a basic need of food and energy; it affords us the opportunity to get to know others better. It helps us to get to know our family better by taking time for one another. It helps us get to know our priests better when we invite them for dinner or a cup of coffee. If we take the time it also helps us get to know neighbors better. The interaction of sharing a meal helps us grow in love.

Do you remember the first time you fell in love? Time seemed to have no meaning except for your parents who wanted to know where you were and what you were doing. When we spend the gift of our time on somebody it lets them know how special they are to us. The same gift of love awaits us at Mass each time we celebrate. It draws us into that loving relationship with the Lord. It nourishes our spirit.

Priests have the awesome responsibility of using their time, skills, talents and experiences to bring us into relationship with the Lord and one another. To the extent you get to know them, it will be a more meaningful experience. Getting to know other parishioners also enhances gathering at the table of the Lord. Taking it one step further, participating in a ministry of the parish, raises it to the level of being a disciple of Jesus. It is the Lord who calls you, feeds you body and soul.

I give thanks to all the priests who have given us this gift of life and love in dedicated service, inviting us to share at the table of the Lord each Sunday.

Ad multos annos!

AMEN

Clergy Index

Rev. Jerry Williams, O. Carm

Rev. Mike Zaniolo

Rev. Bill Zavaski

Index of Recipes

2nd Helpings

Second Helpings

The reason for this title is natural. When you like a meal or dessert and wish for a portion more you ask for a "second helping".

In this last chapter to Burnt Offerings I have introduced about thirty-four new recipes and fifteen new contributors. Some of these recipes were accidentally left out of the first printing, others are new, all are tempting from as far away as Germany and Slovakia. From Russian Chicken Tsaritsa to Polish Chlodnik (borscht), contributors ranging from a Joliet bishop, many priests and the only monsignor, make this chapter most inviting.

This brings the total clergy represented in this book to 93 priests, 1 monsignor, 8 bishops and 3 popes.

Those who purchased the first copy may view the new recipes on my website, BurntOfferings06.com. Comments may also be offered regarding the recipes and your success or difficulties on the website.

As time permits I will expand the website with pictures of the different recipes as I make them or as readers who try these recipes take pictures and send them to me and space permits. Pictures may be sent to: BurntOfferings06@aol.com

Orders for additional books may also be sent to either the website or web address or by calling St. George Rectory, 708-532-2243. Parishes or non-profit organizations who wish to purchase the books for sale may call or write for pricing and terms of sale.

Get to know your priests. Talk to your young boys about their potential vocation to priesthood. If you know of a young man whom you think would be a good priest, approach him and let him know your thoughts. You may be the messenger God has sent to plant the seeds of a new vocation. Priests are not extraordinary men. We are ordinary men, who answered the call to serve. We do the best we can with the skills and talents with which we have been blessed.

Just as a recipe is only as good as the ingredients and the love and attention with which they are combined, so too a parish is only as good as the parishioners and the love and commitment that bring them together as one.

Bon Apetit !
Fr. Ken Fleck

Pizza Dough

3 c. flour

3 t. baking powder
1 t. salt
3 T. olive oil or vegetable oil
1 c. milk
2 t. olive oil

Sift together flour, baking powder, and salt. Place in a large bowl. Add milk and olive oil. Mix by hand or metal mixing spoon until dough leaves sides and is soft and pliable. Take dough from bowl and knead on a well-floured board or clean surface.

Let dough rest for five minutes. On a lightly floured surface roll dough to fit a cookie sheet with an edge. If children are helping do not worry about perfection.

The dough may not stretch to the edges. That's okay. Roll as thick or thin as you like. Brush dough with olive oil, especially the edges so they will not burn.

Top with favorite sauce then toppings (p. 56). Finish with a layer of your favorite cheeses. Shredded cheese will melt more evenly. Be creative and try combinations you like. Remember a pizza is a hot open-faced sandwich. This will help you to try new combination.

Bake in a 425 degree oven 20-25 minutes. Time will vary with the amount of ingredients you have used.

—Fr. Ken Fleck

Auntie Hotcha's Cheesecake

Crust

Get any style of brand-name graham cracker crumbs and follow the directions on the box. Spoon into 11" x 8" x 1" (deep) pan and press to bottom and sides. Let cool.

Filling

2-1/2 packages of Philadelphia cream cheese (20 oz.)
    (soften at room temperature)

1/2 c. sugar

2 eggs

1 t. vanilla extract

Blend sugar into softened cream cheese, mix in one egg at a time, add vanilla and mix until completely blended. Spoon filling into cooled crust and even out. Bake for 20 minutes at 350 degrees and let cool.

Topping

1 c. Breakstone sour cream

1/4 c. sugar

1 t. vanilla extract

Blend and spread lightly on top of cooled cake. Bake for 5 minutes at 350 degrees. Let cool and store in refrigerator.

Note: This cheesecake may also be made in a low-fat, low cholesterol form using light cream cheese and sour cream, egg beaters, and pour able Nutrasweet in the same proportions as their high-fat, high cholesterol cousins. There is not significant difference in taste.

—*Rev. Phil Cyscon*

Bean Soup

3 lbs. favorite dried beans
(You can also mix 1 lb. of three different beans or any combination)
1 ham bone with some meat on it or 2 lbs. smoked turkey
1 c. coarsely chopped green onions
1 c. coarsely chopped red onion
1 c. coarsely chopped white onion
1 bunch of celery coarsely chopped
6 to 8 carrots peeled and chopped
1 green pepper diced
2 T. ketchup
2 T. red wine vinegar
2 T. lemon juice
1 large tomato diced
1 clove of garlic chopped fine
6 whole cloves
Salt and pepper to taste
4 to 5 quarts water

Wash and check beans for any stones or debris. Place beans in a large pot. Cover with water and let soak overnight. The next day throw out the soaking water. Rinse beans. Place in a large pot with 5 quarts of water over high heat until water boils. Reduce heat to simmer. Add smoked meat or ham bone, onions, celery, carrots, and green pepper. Cover and simmer for one hour.

Add ketchup, vinegar, lemon juice, tomato, garlic, cloves, Continue to simmer for 30 to 60 minutes longer until desired tenderness of beans.

Add salt and pepper to taste.

—Rev. Chris Reuter, O Carm.

Brownies

4 squares unsweetened chocolate	2/3 c. butter
1-1/2 c. flour	2 c. sugar
4 eggs	1 t. vanilla
1 t. salt	1 t. baking powder

Microwave and melt butter and chocolate. Allow to cool for 15 minutes. Sift together flour, salt, and baking powder. Beat the eggs in a large mixing bowl. Stir in chocolate/butter mixture. Add 1 c. sugar and flour. Stir until well blended, about 2 minutes. Place batter into a greased and floured 9 x 13 pan. Bake 350 degrees 25 to 30 minutes.

Remove from oven and allow to cool completely. Brownies are most easily cut with a plastic knife. The baked brownie will not stick to a plastic knife.

Walnuts or other nuts may be added for variety. You may substitute mint extract for vanilla extract.

—Fr. Ken Fleck

Bruschetta

Bruschetta comes in many different varieties in Italy and local restaurants. Be creative adding and exchanging different flavors with basil, oregano, garlic, olives, and onion. This is basically garlic bread dressed up. If you prefer a mild garlic flavor rather than garlic in your mixture, rub your toasted bread rounds with a clove of garlic.

**3 medium ripe tomato or
   5 Roma tomatoes**

1/2 c. black olives

**1/2 c. finely chopped fresh basil leaves
Extra virgin olive oil**

1 loaf Italian or French bread

**1 t. minced garlic (two
   cloves)**

1 medium sweet onion

2 t. Italian seasoning

Dice tomato into small cubes. Chop black olives and onion into a small dice. Smash and dice or mince garlic. Mix all ingredients. The juice from the tomato should be enough to make the mixture moist. If you like you can add a little olive oil to bind the ingredients.

Slice your bread into rounds one-half to one inch thick. Brush lightly with olive oil, Place on cookie sheet. Broil on top rack of oven until slightly toasted, 2 to 3 minutes, Remove toasted rounds. Place on a serving plate surrounding a decorative bowl into which you have placed the bruschetta.

You may also serve this to your guests with the bruscetta already on the toasted rounds. Optional garnish is with grated Parmesan cheese.

—Rev. Ken Fleck

Bryndza Dumplings

2 lbs. potatoes
1 lb. bryndza (sheep cheese, cottage cheese)
(Bryndza is available at ethnic food stores and Bozak's in Chicago)
1/2 lb. smoked bacon
1 egg
1-1/2 c. flour
1 to 2 t. salt
3 to 4 T. butter
1 medium onion diced
milk

Boil potatoes with skins on for 15 to 20 minutes, until fork tender. After potatoes are done peel potatoes. Mash cooked potatoes. After they are mashed and cooled, add one beaten egg and gradually add flour kneading until dough doesn't stick to the bowl. Add salt to taste during kneading. Break off small thimble size bits of dough and drop into boiling water or you can force the dough through a large ricer into the boiling water. Boil for approximately 2 to 3 minutes. Dumplings will float when done. Once all the dumplings are done, drain, allow to dry, and add the butter while they are hot. Stir to coat evenly. Set aside.

Cook the bacon crisp. Drain on paper towels. Crumble bacon. Reserve 2 T. bacon fat. Sauté the onion in this fat for five minutes until translucent and tender. Prepare bryndza with a little milk until it is the consistency of cooked soupy oatmeal. Mix bryndza into the dumplings. Top with bacon bits and onion. Enjoy your meal.

—Rev. Eugen Rybansky
Diocese of Nitra, Slovakia

Chicken al Forno

1 lb. chicken breast fillet

2 medium white onions

1 sprig fresh rosemary or 1 t. dry

1 lemon, cut into wedges

salt and pepper to taste

4 medium potatoes

olive oil

1/4 c. pitted black olives, sliced or whole

Cut chicken breast fillets into cubes. Slice potatoes into wedges. Cut onions into medium size pieces. Place the chicken, potatoes, and onions into a large bowl. Add a dash of salt and pepper to taste. Add rosemary, separating and sprinkling over the other ingredients. Lightly coat all the ingredients with olive oil. Place all ingredients into an oven safe casserole dish. Cover and bake in pre-heated oven 350 degrees for 30 minutes. Add black olives and lemon wedges. Bake for another 10 minutes.

—Rev. Ludger Molitor
Diocese of Essen, Germany

Chicken Ala Capers

2 whole boneless, skinless chicken breasts

salt and white pepper to taste   **1 T. light olive oil**

1 T. butter   **3 T. minced shallots**

1 T. chopped garlic

4 ripe plum tomatoes, cut into small cubes

1/2 c. dry white wine   **1/4 c. drained capers**

2 T. red wine vinegar   **1 T. tomato paste**

2 T. fresh tarragon   **2 t. celery flakes**

Season chicken with salt and pepper. Heat oil and butter in a large, heavy-bottom, non-reactive skillet. Add chicken breasts in a single layer. Sauté over medium-high heat, turning pieces often until lightly browned, about 5 minutes.

Add shallots and garlic around the chicken. Cook briefly, about 2 minutes, add tomatoes, wine, capers, vinegar, celery flakes, tomato paste, and tarragon. Stir to dissolve brown particles adhering to the bottom of the skillet and to blend all ingredients.

Bring mixture to a boil. Cover and simmer 5 minutes or until chicken is done. Garnish with parsley and serve.

—Rev. Bob Tonelli

Chicken Lemon

4 to 6 boneless, skinless chicken breasts

1/2 c. olive oil	1 T. butter
2 eggs	1/2 c. chicken broth
1 c. milk	2 c. dry white wine
1/4 t. salt	2 to 3 t. lemon juice
1/2 t. pepper	1 to 2 t. cornstarch (optional)
1 clove garlic, crushed	1 lemon thinly sliced
1-1/2 c. seasoned bread crumbs	1 T. capers, drained

Flatten the chicken breasts slightly with a mallet or rolling pin. In a shallow dish, stir together the eggs, milk, pepper, and garlic. In a second dish spread the seasoned bread crumbs. Dip each chicken piece into the egg mixture and then cover in bread crumbs and set aside to dry. In a large frying pan heat the olive oil along with the butter over medium heat. Add the chicken breasts. Fry the chicken breasts until golden brown. Drain the chicken breasts on paper towels. In a large baking pan, arrange the chicken breasts in a single layer. In a separate mixing bowl, stir together the chicken broth, dry white wine and lemon juice. If desired you can stir in 1 to 2 t. cornstarch to thicken the liquid. Pour the liquid over the chicken breasts. Cover with foil. Bake at 350 degrees for 25 to 30 minutes. Garnish with lemon slices and capers to taste.

This dish goes well with white rice made with chicken broth rather than water, sautéed onions and portabella mushrooms.

—Rev. John Noga

Chicken Marsala

6 medium boneless, skinless chicken breasts

1 t. garlic powder

2 t. finely chopped fresh basil

2 eggs

1/2 c. olive oil

1-1/2 c. flour

1 T. butter

1/3 c. grated Parmesan cheese

Flatten the chicken breasts slightly with a mallet or rolling pin. Beat the eggs in a bowl with 2 T. water. In a separate bowl, mix flour, cheese, garlic powder, and basil. Dip the chicken breasts one at a time in the egg wash and then coat with the flour mixture. Heat the oil with the butter in a frying pan and brown the chicken over medium heat, 3 minutes each side.

Marsala Sauce

1/2 stick butter

1 c. Marsala wine

1 medium red onion

1/2 c. chicken broth

1 (8-oz.) pkg. fresh sliced mushrooms

1 t. finely chopped fresh basil

1 to 2 T. cornstarch

In a separate pan, melt the butter and sauté the onion and mushrooms for just a few minutes until the begin to become tender. Add the Marsala wine and chicken broth along with cornstarch for thickening. Let the sauce simmer on low heat for about 15 minutes. Place the chicken breasts in a single layer in a casserole or baking pan. Pour the Marsala sauce over the chicken breasts and sprinkle with basil. Bake at 350 for about 30 minutes.

You may also substitute veal medallions for the chicken breasts to make veal Marsala.

—Rev. John Noga

Chicken Tsaritsa (Russian)

4 chicken breasts, split and boned

1-1/2 c. sour cream or plain yogurt

1/4 c. lemon juice

2 t. salt

2 t. garlic salt or 4 cloves minced garlic

2 t. Worcestershire sauce

1/4 t. paprika

1/4 t. pepper

fresh white bread crumbs (ground in blender or food processor)

1/2 lb. unsalted sweet butter

fresh or dried chives

chopped fresh dill

Combine in a glass container: sour cream (yogurt), lemon juice, and seasonings. Roll chicken breasts in mixture, cover and refrigerate overnight. (Once coated you may place all the chicken breasts and marinade in a large plastic baggie sealed in the refrigerator.)

Remove chicken, roll in bread crumbs. Retain as much of the marinade as possible. Place chicken breasts in lightly buttered baking dish. Pour half of the remaining butter over the chicken. Bake 45 minutes at 325 degrees. Pour remaining butter over the chicken and bake 15 minutes more. Garnish with fresh dill and chives sprinkled over the chicken breasts and serve.

Serves 8. Excellent with kasha or couscous

—Rev. Andrew Luczak

Chlodnik (Cold Summer Borscht) (Polish)

1/2 gallon of buttermilk

1 to 1-1/2 bunches green onions

2 bunches of radishes

3 cucumbers

10 hard boiled eggs

5 1-lb. jars of beets and juice

2 lbs. raw shrimp

3 c. fresh chopped dill

2 T. salt

sour cream to taste

Pour 1/2 gallon of buttermilk into a large bowl or pan. Add 1 to1-1/2 bunches of green onion chopped, 2 bunches of radishes thinly sliced, 3 cucumbers (remove seeds) chopped small, 10 hard boiled eggs finely chopped, 5 1-lb. jars of beets (sliced shoestring style), Add the juice.

Cook 2 lbs of shrimp with 3 c. dill and 2 T. salt. Cut shrimp into small pieces and add to soup. Discard the dill weed Garnish with sour cream and fresh snipped dill.

Serve with black rye bread.

—Rev. Andrew Luczak

"Did Fr. Fleck really get the recipe for the "Bread of Life" from Jesus?

Official Eucharistic Bread

2-1/2 c. whole wheat flour

1 c. water

Mix into a soft pliable dough. Roll onto a floured surface to only 1/4 inch thick. Place on a cookie sheet. Score with a pizza wheel. Let it rest for 10 to 15 minutes before baking. Bake 350 degrees for 15 minutes. Do not over bake or you will have a hard cracker texture. Serves 100 to 125 pieces.

Unofficial Eucharistic Bread

(This represents an effort to make bread that is symbolic with ingredients from the Old Testament as well as inclusive of indigenous ingredients.)

1 c. white flour

1 c. whole wheat flour

1/2 c. corn meal (represents an indigenous grain of the New World)

4 T. honey (the earliest sweetening agent and listed in the Old Testament)

1/2 t. baking soda (we are to be the leaven in society)

1/2 t. salt ("You are the salt of the earth")

1-1/2 T. olive oil (a sign of healing)

3/4 c. milk (our first food in this life)

Sift together dry ingredients twice. In a large bowl mix together the honey, oil and milk. Add flour and knead into a soft dough. Allow to rest five minutes. Separate into two equal parts. On a lightly floured surface flatten with the palm of your hand until you have two small discs only about 1/4 inch thick. You can use a rolling pin too. Place dough on a cookie sheet. Score with a pizza wheel into bite size pieces, crisscross pattern. Bake 350 degrees for 20 minutes. Serves 100 to 125. Do not over bake.

—*Fr. Ken Fleck*

Fettuccine Alfredo

1 - 8 oz. pkg. cream cheese

3 oz. parmesan cheese

1/2 stick margarine

1/2 c. milk

1 pkg. fettuccine

Combine all ingredients in a medium sauce pan. Bring ingredients to a simmer over medium heat stirring to blend ingredients and avoid burning. Prepare 8 oz. of fettuccine according to package directions.

(You may use any pasta shape you prefer.) After cooking pasta do not rinse. Combine pasta with Alfredo sauce in a large serving dish.

Options:

You may add chicken breast slices. Brown the chicken and cook thoroughly before adding. You may also add cooked shrimp.

—*Rev. John Fearon*

Giant Chocolate Chip Cookies

2 sticks sweet butter, softened

1 c. brown sugar

3/4 c. granulated sugar

2 eggs

1 t. vanilla extract

1 t. salt

2 -1/4 c. flour

1 t. baking soda

12 ounces semisweet chocolate chips

Preheat oven to 325 degrees. Grease a cookie sheet. Cream butter and both sugars together until light and fluffy. Add eggs and vanilla and mix well. Sift dry ingredients together and stir in, mixing toughly. Add chocolate chips to batter. Using an ice cream scoop for portioning the dough, drop a ball onto the cookie sheet. Wet your hand with water and flatten the cookie out to a five inch round. Bake on the middle rack of the oven for 15 to17 minutes. Remove from oven while centers are still slightly soft. Cool on the baking sheet for 5 minutes before transferring to a rack to cool.

You can vary the recipe by:

Adding 1 c. finely chopped walnuts

Adding 1 c. shredded coconut

Substituting 1 t. mint extract for the vanilla extract

—*Rev. Mike Gallagher*

Guacamole

2 ripe avocados (Haas preferred)
3 tbsp. minced shallot or onion
1 small tomato, peeled, seeded, diced
1 tsp. dried cilantro
1/4 tsp. salt
dash of lime juice

Combine all ingredients. Mash with a fork. Taste and add more salt if needed. Serve immediately.

—*Rev. Darrio Boscutti*

Holiday Punch Flambé

(Serves a whole part of holiday merrymakers)

1 quart bourbon	1 pint rum
1 pint Cointreau (orange liqueur)	1 quart water
1 c. sugar	3 to 5 cinnamon sticks, to taste
2 oranges sliced	2 lemons sliced
juice of two oranges	juice of two lemons

<u>Caution: This is a flaming punch</u>.

In a large metal pot add all ingredients. Gradually heat to just below the
boiling point. Carefully ignite the vapors with a long-handled ignitor.

CAUTION ! As the mixture heats the vapors are VERY flammable. Flame
may appear calm in a deep metal pot but will flare up when poured into
cups.

For safety:

- —Use only a metal ladle. A plastic one will melt.
- —Wear a cooking glove to avoid burns.
- —Cook and serve only from a metal pot.
- —Serve in heat proof cups or coffee mugs.

—*Rev. Rich Homa*

Lost Lake Peach Almond Crisp

6 c. sliced peaches	2 c. brown sugar
1 c. flour	1 c. rolled oats
1 to 2 c. slivered almonds	2 t. cinnamon
2 t. nutmeg	1 t. salt
3/4 c. melted butter	2 t. vanilla
4 oz. almond paste	

In a bowl stir together dry ingredients. Stir in butter and vanilla. Grease a 9 x 13 baking pan and press a thin layer of mixture on the bottom. Add a layer of peaches and mixture. Dot with almond paste. Then top with the remaining mixture, lightly pressing into place. Bake at 350 degrees covered for 45 min. Uncover and bake for 15 minutes more.

—Rev. Ken Fleck

Marinated Vegetables

Mix:

1/2 c. cooking oil
1/2 c. vinegar
3/4 c. sugar
1 t. salt
1 t. celery seed

1 can (16 oz.) drained cut green beans
1 can (16 oz.) drained corn
1 can (16 oz.) drained carrots
1 can (16 oz.) drained corn
1 large onion cut in strips
1 large bell pepper cut in strips

Pour mix over vegetables and marinate overnight. Use fork to toss. Serve in a decorative bowl or served individually on lettuce leaves.

—Rev. Ken Fleck

Mashed Sweet Potatoes

3 c. cooked mashed potatoes
1/2 c. sugar - less if you desire
1/4 c. milk
1 t. vanilla
1/3 c. margarine (melted)
2 eggs (beaten)

Combine ingredients above, mix well and pour into lightly greased eight-inch casserole dish.

1 c. flaked coconut
1 c. firmly packed brown sugar (scant)
1/3 c. margarine (melted)
1 c. chopped pecans (without salt)

Combine and sprinkle over top.

Bake in preheated 375 degree oven approximately 25 minutes, or until golden brown.

—Rev. Jeffrey Grob

Oatmeal Cookies

3/4 c. vegetable shortening

1/2 c. granulated sugar

1/4 c. water

3 c. oatmeal (uncooked)

1 t. salt

1 c. firmly packed brown sugar

1 egg

1 t. vanilla

1 c. all purpose flour

1/2 t. soda

Preheat oven to 350 degrees. Beat together shortening, sugar, egg, water, and vanilla till creamy. Add combined remaining ingredients, mix well. Drop rounded teaspoonfuls onto greased cookie sheet. Bake at 350 degrees for 12 to 15 minutes. For variety add chopped nuts, raisins, or chocolate chips. Makes about 5 dozen cookies.

—Rev. Ken Fleck

Old Fashion Vegetable Beef Soup

2 T. oil

1 medium onion, diced

1 28 oz. stewed tomatoes

3 carrots, sliced

1/2 lb. green beans, sliced

  black pepper, to taste

  hot pepper sauce, to taste

1 clover garlic

1 lb. lean beef, cubed

2 c. beef stock

1/2 lb. mushroom, sliced

4 ribs celery, sliced

  cayenne pepper, to taste

2 medium potatoes, diced

In a Dutch oven, heat oil and lightly brown onions, garlic and meat. Add tomatoes and beef stock. Bring to a boil, then reduce to a simmer. Add carrots, mushrooms, green beans and celery. Season and taste with black pepper, cayenne and hot pepper sauce.

Cover and simmer 45 minutes. Add potatoes and cook until tender. Add more water during cooking if necessary.

Serving Ideas: Serve with corn bread

Notes: Salt may be added but celery usually supplies enough.

    Soup is better after setting awhile.

    Soup freezes well but not the potatoes.

—Rev. Mike Gallagher

Orange Cookies

3 c. sifted flour

1 t. salt

1/2 t. baking soda

1 c. butter

1 c. sugar

1 - 6 oz. can frozen orange juice concentrate, thawed

Sift together flour, salt and baking soda. Set aside. In a mixer, cream butter, and sugar for about 7 minutes. Add orange concentrate and mix until well blended. Stir in dry ingredients. Wrap dough in plastic wrap and chill in refrigerator for two hours or until ready.

Divide dough into four parts. Roll one part at a time to 1/8 - inch thick on lightly floured surface or waxed paper. Cut out shapes with cookie cutter or circles with a drinking glass. Place cookies on lightly greased cookie sheet or parchment paper lined cookie sheet. Bake 400 degrees for 7 to 9 minutes until lightly browned. Allow to cool for three minutes before removing to cooling rack.

—Rev. Ken Fleck

Pam's Fresh Tomato Salad

2 lbs. tomatoes (about six medium)

8 oz. pkg. Feta cheese, crumbled

8 oz. bacon (about ten slices)

2 T. water

1/4 c. balsamic vinegar

1 T. Dijon style mustard

1 medium sweet onion, very thinly sliced

2 T. Greek seasoning

1/2 c. olive oil

2 T. honey

Wash tomatoes and slice into 1/4 inch thick slices. Peel and thinly slice onion, set aside. Chop bacon into one-inch pieces. Fry until crispy. Drain on paper towel. In a large bowl mix Greek seasoning in water. Let stand for a few minutes. Add olive oil, vinegar, honey, and mustard. Whisk well. Add onion and crumble Feta cheese into the bowl. Arrange tomato slices nicely on salad plates. Just before serving, sprinkle bacon bits on top of the tomatoes then pour a small ladle of dressing on top of each serving.

—Rev. John Kuzinskas

Pasta with Rappini and Chickpeas

1 bunch of rappini (broccoli-rabe)
6 cloves of garlic finely chopped
1/2 sweet onion finely chopped
1/4 t. red pepper flakes
1 c. canned (cooked) chickpeas drained
3 T. chopped flatleaf parsley
4 T. olive oil
2 c. dry, small penne or rotini pasta
1 T. fresh lemon juice
salt and fresh ground pepper to taste

Chop rappini, onion and garlic. Cook rappini in 3 quarts of salted, boiling water for 4 minutes. Reserve the water. Scoop rappini out and drain. Cook the pasta in the water for 7 minutes. In a large skillet, add olive oil. Lightly sauté onion for 3 minutes over medium heat, add the garlic and red pepper flakes. Saute another 2 minutes. Do not let garlic burn! Add chickpeas and pasta, stirring and turning to coat evenly. Add parsley and lemon juice, salt and pepper to taste.

Stir and cook for 2 minutes more to heat all ingredients and coat. Garnish with freshly grated Parmesan cheese.

Option:

For an interesting Asian variation, add 1 t. of Chinese oyster sauce (omitting the lemon and lessening the salt.)

—Rev. Andrew Luczak

Poppy Seed Cake

Duncan Hines yellow cake mix
vanilla instant pudding (3.4 oz pkg.)
5 eggs
1 c. sour half and half
1/3 c. soft butter
1 can Solo Poppy Seed filling

Mix all together, put in greased bundt pan or tube pan and bake for 1 hr. and 15 min. at 350 degrees. Insert a toothpick to test for doneness. When toothpick comes out clear of any sticky dough, cake is done. Allow to cool before turning over to remove from pan or cake will split apart while warm.

—*Rev. Ken Fleck*

Pork Chop in Beer Marinade

8 boneless pork chops cut no less than 1 to 1-1/2 inch thick
1 t. salt
1/2 t. black pepper or cayenne pepper
1/2 t. paprika
1 medium onion
1 can beer

Arrange the pork chops in a baking pan. Season each chop with salt, pepper and paprika to taste. Top each chop with an onion slice. Pour one can of beer over the chops. Cover the pan with foil or plastic wrap and refrigerate for at least one hour. Spray your grill with vegetable oil and raise the heat to high. Brown the chops 2 minutes on each side. Reduce the heat to low and let cook 8 to 10 minutes.

As the chops are cooking baste with the left over marinade. The beer marinade keeps the chops moist. (You can also use your favorite barbecue sauce for the last few minutes.)

—*Rev. John Noga*

Potato Chip Cookies

(This is a great cookie to make from a collection of all those potato chips nobody wants to eat at the bottom of the bag. Save them in a baggie until you have 1 cup for this cookie.)

1/2 c. butter or margarine

1/2 c. sugar

2 t. vanilla

1-1/2 c. flour

1 c. crumbled potato chips

Pre-heat oven to 325 degrees. In a mixed cream butter and sugar. Add vanilla. Stir in flour and add potato chips. Drop onto ungreased cookie sheet 1 t. at a time. Bake 10 to12 minutes or until golden brown.

—*Rev. Ken Fleck*

Pumpkin Loaves

2 c. sugar

1 - 16 oz. can pumpkin

2 eggs

1/2 c. oil

2 c. flour

1 1/2 t. baking soda

1 t. cinnamon

3/4 t. allspice

1/2 t. salt

1 c. chopped dates

1 c. chopped walnuts or pecans

Preheat the oven to 350 degrees. Combine sugar, pumpkin, and eggs. Beat until well blended. Add oil and beat. Blend in flour, soda, cinnamon, allspice, and salt. Stir in dates and nuts. Divide batter equally among 4 2-cup mini loaf pans. Bake in preheated 350 degree oven for about 50 minutes. Cool on rack.

—*Rev. Ken Fleck*

Rum Cookies

Filling

1 lb. walnuts, ground

2 lb. jar apricot jam

2 c. of sugar per lb. of ground nuts

Mix ground nuts and sugar. Set aside.

Dough

4 c. flour	1/2 lb. soft butter
3 T. sugar	1 egg
2 yolks	1/2 c. warm milk
1 oz. yeast	2 T. rum

Mix flour and butter. Mix sugar and eggs. Dissolve yeast in warm milk. Combine the preceding ingredients. Divide dough in 6 parts. Let dough stand for half an hour. Roll out each part on a lightly floured surface to 10 x 15 rectangles. Place one piece of dough in 10 x 15 inch pan. Spread jam on dough. Sprinkle nut and sugar mixture over it. Repeat three times. Bake at 350 degrees for 30 minutes. Let cool, then cut in diamond shape. Yields 2 -10 x 15 pans each 3 layers high. Rum can be added to dough or mixed into the filling or both if you prefer.

—Rev. Ken Fleck

Sausage Dip Recipe

4 Italian sausage links (mild or hot)

2 – 8 oz. pkgs. of cream cheese

1 can (16 oz.) Rotel diced tomatoes

Remove Italian sausage from the casing. In a large skillet over medium heat prepare the sausage until thoroughly cooked and broken into small pieces of cooked meat. Drain excess fat. Add the cream cheese and continue cooking on low heat until the cheese is melted. Add drained can of Rotel until all the ingredients are cooked and incorporated.

Serve with small crackers. If not used immediately, place in an oven safe dish and reheat at 350 degrees until warm.

—Msgr. Kenneth Velo

Simple Salmon

In order to prepare this recipe, you need only a few simple ingredients:

A large, heavy frying pan or pan with a lid
salmon fillets
white wine (preferably a dry Chardonnay)
lemons
capers
parsley

In order to prepare the Simple Salmon, pour 1/2 bottle of Chardonnay into frying pan and let the salmon fillets soak overnight, several hours, or not at all. While salmon marinates, add slices of lemon, a couple of teaspoons of capers, and some squeezed lemon juice. When ready to cook, place the salmon over the stove. Turn the burner on high or as high a flame you can get. Put the lid on. Wait for ten minutes. Within a couple of minutes the salmon will begin to boil (poach). You may need to ease off the lid to allow steam to evaporate. After ten minutes, turn off the heat and remove the salmon from the frying pan. Garnish with fresh lemon slices, capers and parsley. This meal can be served with asparagus and rice.

—Rev. Scott Donahue

Sweet Fruit Dip

Ingredients
crème de menthe to taste
1 - 16 oz. tub Cool Whip

Mix the crème de menthe with the Cool Whip. Place in a decorative bowl. Garnish with a Maraschino cherry. Cover and keep in the refrigerator until ready to serve. To serve slice large fruit into bite size pieces and place smaller fruit in a decorative pattern on a large platter. Place the bowl of flavored Cool Whip in the center and serve.

—Bishop Roger Kaffer
Diocese of Joliet

Veal Alla Tonelli

1 c. white wine

3 stalks chopped celery

1 bunch chopped (fine) parsley

1 medium onion chopped fine

2 cloves of minced garlic

1 fresh tomato chopped

1 - 6 oz. can tomato paste

1-1/2 to 2 lbs. of excellent veal pounded thin about 1/2 inch thick

3 bay leaves

3 t. ground thyme

3 beef bouillon cubes

salt and pepper to taste

1/4 c. butter

3 t. vegetable oil

3 t. oregano

1 c. chicken broth

In a skillet, over medium-high heat, place the olive oil and 1 t. butter. Sear the veal quickly about 1 minute on each side. Set aside. In the same pan reduce the heat to medium. Saute the onion, about 3 minutes. Add the parsley, celery, tomatoes, tomato paste, and all other ingredients. Add chicken broth and 1/2 c. water. Return the veal to the skillet. Let simmer about 10 minutes. Garnish with fresh parsley sprigs.

—Rev. Bob Tonelli

WGN Special Bar Cookie

(I created this cookie to thank WGN-TV for their support.)

8 oz. milk chocolate
1 c. Nutella
1 c. roasted walnuts, coarsely chopped
2 c. granola
2 c. crispy rice cereal

Roasted walnuts

Place 1 c. walnut pieces in a non-stick skillet over medium heat.

This takes 3 to 5 minutes. Do not leave unattended. Walnut pieces need to be stirred or flipped over about every 30 seconds to keep from burning. Place in a separate bowl to stop the cooking until ready to use.

Melt milk chocolate in a microwave safe dish on high for 60 seconds.

Stir and if not melted give another 15 seconds in the microwave repeatedly until it is easily stirred to a smooth consistency.

Add the Nutella to the melted chocolate. (Nutella is a hazelnut chocolate spread.) Stir to blend the two chocolates. Add the walnut pieces, stir. Add the granola and crispy rice cereal.

Using an 8 x 8-inch pan, or round cake pans or any decorative shape you want, line it with waxed paper. Press the cookie mixture into the pan or mold. Allow to set and cool completely before removing from pan and cutting with a sharp knife.

Options:

—Cookies may be dropped onto waxed paper and sprinkled with more walnut pieces. You may also garnish this cookie with a drizzle of white chocolate.

—For a denser cookie increase the granola and decrease the rice cereal.

—White or dark chocolate may be substituted for milk chocolate. You can use bags of chocolate chip pieces (12 oz.) and increase the cereal or granola by 1 c. each to adjust for the increased chocolate. Also increase the Nutella by 1/2 to 1 cup. Be creative!

—*Rev. Ken Fleck*

Clergy Index